ERWIN CHEMERINSKY

THE SUPREME COURT
Taking Sides

OCTOBER TERM 2024

AMERICAN BAR ASSOCIATION
Judicial Division

Cover design by Mary Anne Kulchawik/ABA Design

Printed in the United States of America.

29 28 27 26 25 5 4 3 2 1

ISBN 978-1-63905-708-5

Discounts are available for books ordered in bulk. Special consideration is given to state bars, CLE programs, and other bar-related organizations. Inquire at Book Publishing, ABA Publishing, American Bar Association, 321 N. Clark Street, Chicago, Illinois 60654-7598.

www.shopABA.org

For my grandchildren,
Andrew, Sarah, and Amy

Contents

Preface

This is the fifth year in which I have the great pleasure of writing a book for the American Bar Association summarizing the just-completed Supreme Court term. I am grateful to Jeffrey Salyards at the ABA for making this possible and to Bob Edmunds and Herb Dixon for initially suggesting this series.

As I have said in past years, my goal in this book is to present the cases as clearly as I can and to explain their implications. My hope is to do this in a neutral manner, without evaluating them or editorializing. I certainly have views about many of them and cannot pretend that they do not sometimes affect my presentation of the cases. That is especially true about many of the cases this term—nationwide injunctions, bans on gender-affirming care for transgender youth, recognizing a First Amendment right of parents to remove their children from public school instruction that they find objectionable on religious grounds. My objective, though, is to present the cases as fairly as I can and leave my normative judgments to be expressed in other places.

I want to express my great appreciation to my research assistants—Eleanor Gartstein, Laith Hourani, Anagha Iyer, and Gary Soiseth—for their terrific assistance. And as always, my wonderful executive assistant, Whitney Mello, was invaluable. Catherine Fisk and Alex Chemerinsky talked through many of the ideas in the book.

It was another very important term in the Supreme Court, and I feel privileged to have this opportunity to write about it.

Chapter 1

Introduction

Taking Sides

At a time when the United States is more ideologically divided than at any time since Reconstruction, what will it mean to have a Supreme Court that has so consistently and solidly come down on one side of that divide? The Court's October Term 2024, which released its last decisions on Friday, June 27, 2025, included a number of cases to the justices that posed politically controversial issues concerning the actions of President Donald Trump and also the "culture wars." Time and again in these cases, the Court, in 6–3 decisions, came down on the conservative side. Liberals will decry this, and conservatives will applaud it, but no one can deny that this was a year of the Supreme Court taking sides.

Perhaps the most important case of the term was a stunning restriction on the power of federal courts to restrain unconstitutional actions by the President and the federal government. In *Trump v. CASA*, the Supreme Court held that no longer can federal courts issue nationwide injunctions to stop unconstitutional presidential actions and federal laws.[1] The case arose in the context of President Trump's executive order to largely end birthright citizenship. Three federal district courts declared this unconstitutional and issued nationwide injunctions. Each of the federal courts of appeals affirmed. The Supreme Court did not rule on the constitutionality of the executive order, but did hold that the federal courts lacked the authority to issue the nationwide injunctions.

The Supreme Court, in a 6–3 ruling split along ideological lines, said that federal courts lack the power to issue such orders. Justice Amy Coney Barrett, writing for the conservative justices, declared that such universal injunctions "likely exceed the equitable authority that Congress has granted to federal courts."[2] Justice Clarence Thomas, in a concurring opinion, put this succinctly: "Today puts an end to the 'increasingly common' practice of federal courts issuing universal injunctions."[3]

Justices Sonia Sotomayor and Ketanji Brown Jackson each wrote blistering dissents. Justice Sotomayor said: "No right is safe in the new legal regime the Court creates. Today, the threat is to birthright citizenship. Tomorrow, a different administration may try to seize firearms from law-abiding citizens or prevent people of certain faiths from gathering to worship. . . . That holding renders constitutional guarantees meaningful in name only for any individuals who are not parties to a lawsuit. Because I will not be complicit in so grave an attack on our system of law, I dissent."[4] Justice Jackson wrote in her dissent, "The Court's decision to permit the Executive to violate the Constitution with respect to anyone who has not yet sued is an existential threat to the rule of law."[5]

Repeatedly, though not in every instance, as discussed in Chapter 13, the Court upheld the actions of the Trump administration that had been enjoined by the lower courts. These matters came to the Supreme Court on its emergency docket, often called the "shadow docket." The cases are decided without the benefit of briefing and oral argument, often with no opinions or only very short explanations.

An example of great judicial deference to President Trump occurred on Monday, June 23, in *Department of Homeland Security v. D.V.D.*[6] A federal district court had issued a preliminary injunction to keep the Trump administration from deporting individuals to South Sudan. Federal law is specific as to where people can be deported to; only if no alternative exists, does the government have the power to pick its own place. It was clear that the Trump administration was violating this law. But the Court, once more 6–3, reversed the lower court and ruled for the government. It was stunning that there was no explanation whatsoever from the Court, while Justice Sotomayor wrote a scathing dissent.

This was also a term when the culture wars came to the Court and repeatedly the Court came down on the conservative side. For example, the Court decided *Mahmoud v. Taylor*, which involved a challenge to Montgomery County, Maryland's curriculum about sexuality and gender identity.[7] A group of parents objected on religious grounds, saying that it infringed their free exercise of religion for them to not have notice of the curriculum and the opportunity to opt their children out of the instruction. The Court, 6–3, agreed with the parents.

Never before had the Supreme Court held that mere exposure to materials that parents find objectionable is enough to violate the Constitution. It is unclear what it will mean in practice. Does it mean that schools must give parents notice and the chance to opt out every time evolution is taught, or an English class has a book with witches, or anything some parent might find objectionable on religious grounds?

Yet another case directly from the culture wars was *United States v. Skrmetti*, where the Court upheld, again 6–3, a Tennessee law prohibiting gender-affirming care for transgender youth.[8] Twenty-six states, all with Republican-controlled state legislatures, have adopted such a law. Chief Justice John Roberts writing for the majority stressed that the court should defer to the legislatures on this matter.

These, of course, are only a few of the cases from the term. Each is discussed in detail in subsequent chapters. But by all accounts, they are among the most important of the term. And, like a number of other cases discussed throughout this book, they show a conservative Court that came down solidly on the conservative side of the ideological divide.

By the Numbers

As someone who grew up obsessed with baseball statistics (and still am), I think that a great deal can be learned from looking at the numbers concerning the Supreme Court. The statistics from the term, as always, are very revealing.[9]

Size of the merits docket. The Court decided 56 cases with signed opinions after briefing and oral argument. This seems to be the new normal for the Court. Last year, the Court decided 59 merits cases. In each of the two years prior to that, the Court decided 58 cases. The term before that it was 54, and the year before that it was 52, the smallest number since 1862.

To put this in perspective, in the 1980s, the Court was deciding over 160 cases a year. The smaller docket began when William Rehnquist was Chief Justice. In his last year, October Term 2004, the Court decided 85 cases. When John Roberts went before the Senate Judiciary Committee in the summer of 2005 for his confirmation hearing, he was asked about Rehnquist's smaller docket. He lamented it. Roberts had been a Supreme Court litigator and said that the Court should decide at least 100 cases a year. Never in his 20 years as Chief has the Court come close to the 85 merits cases of Rehnquist's last term. On the other hand, as discussed later, the size of the emergency docket has increased enormously.

One interesting consequence of the smaller docket is that the justices generally write one majority opinion for each month the Court hears oral arguments. No justice this term wrote fewer than five or more than seven majority opinions.

Lack of interest in reviewing state court decisions. Of the 56 decisions, only three were reviewing state court rulings. This is not a one-year phenomena. A year ago, only four decisions were reviewing state court decisions, and the year before that it was five. It certainly means that state court judges can rule knowing that the odds of the Supreme Court granting review in one of their cases is very tiny.

It is not clear why the Court has little interest in reviewing the state courts. It may be that the justices care much more about splits among the federal circuits than they do about disagreements among the state courts. Perhaps they see their role as ensuring uniformity of law applied in the federal courts, with less concern afforded to state courts deciding federal law issues.

Perhaps, too, it may be about the issues that are of most interest to the justices. It is striking that again this term, there were no decisions about the scope of searches under the Fourth Amendment, or the privilege against self-incrimination, or eyewitness identifications, or the confrontation clause. Maybe, also, this reflects a relative lack of interest in criminal procedure among the justices. The paucity of criminal procedure cases may be a product, in part, of not reviewing state court decisions, because the vast majority of criminal prosecutions in the United States occur in state courts.

It is the Roberts Court. After Amy Coney Barrett was confirmed and there were five conservative justices without Roberts' vote, many questioned whether it would still be the John Roberts Court. This was vocalized even more after the Court's decision in *Dobbs v. Jackson Women's Health Center* (2022),[10] where the five other conservative justices overruled *Roe v. Wade* without Roberts joining them in that result.

But in the years since, it is clear that in every way, it really is the Roberts Court. Again this term, Roberts was in the majority more than any other justice: 95 percent of the time. He dissented only twice in cases on the merits docket, and wrote no concurring or dissenting opinions. He was in the majority in all of what can be regarded as the most important decisions of the term. He again wrote the majority opinion in several of the most high profile cases of the term.

The United States Court of Appeals for the Fifth Circuit. Of the 56 decisions, 12, or about 20 percent, were reviewing the U.S. Court of Appeals for the Fifth Circuit. By comparison, the next most frequent were eight decisions reviewing the Fourth Circuit, seven decisions reviewing the Ninth Circuit, and five reviewing the D.C. Circuit.

In 10 of the 12 cases, the Fifth Circuit was reversed. I never have felt that reversal rates should be a basis for criticizing a court of appeals. It is not the role of a court of appeals to try and predict what the Supreme Court will do. And the Supreme Court reversing does not mean it was right and the court of appeals was wrong; it is just that the Supreme Court gets the last word.

But when a disproportionate number of cases come from one circuit and that circuit is reversed most of the time, it says something. When it was the Ninth Circuit that was a large part of the docket and often reversed, it reflected a court that overall was to the left of the Supreme Court. Now, with the Fifth Circuit, it shows a court that is often aggressively pushing the law to the right and going further than even the conservative Roberts

Court wants to. That was certainly true this term. For example, in *Federal Communications Commission v. Consumers Research*, the Fifth Circuit declared a federal law unconstitutional as an excessive delegation of legislative power.[11] Since 1935, not once had the Supreme Court struck down a federal law on that basis.[12] And the Court did not do so in this case, reversing the Fifth Circuit in a 6–3 ruling, with Justice Elena Kagan writing for the Court, and Justices Gorsuch, Thomas, and Alito dissenting.

The growth of the emergency docket. A year ago, the Supreme Court decided 44 matters on its emergency, or often called "shadow," docket. This term, the Court had 113 matters on the emergency docket as of June 27. That is a stunning increase in just one year. Of course, the easiest explanation is the number of petitions involving challenges to President Trump's actions.

I am among those with great concerns about the Court effectively deciding major issues without full briefing and oral argument on its emergency docket.[13] Sometimes the Court decides without even writing an opinion, such as in *Department of Homeland Security v. D.V.D.* mentioned earlier, which allowed the Trump administration to deport individuals to South Sudan despite their not having any connection to that country.[14] It also is troubling that the Court pays little attention to rules restricting appellate review of temporary restraining orders or to the usual standards of appellate review, which limit overturning preliminary injunctions to when there is an abuse of discretion by the trial court. Also, it is unclear what, if any, precedential weight lower courts must give to opinions from the emergency docket.

The ideology of the justices. It is no surprise that the justices who were in agreement the most were Thomas and Alito, 97 percent of the time, and then Sotomayor and Jackson, 94 percent of the time. The former are the most conservative justices, and the latter the most liberal.

It does not take statistics to see that for the most high-profile cases that are ideologically divided, this is a Court that has six conservative justices and three liberal justices. Although just 9 percent of the cases were 6–3, with Justices Sotomayor, Kagan, and Jackson dissenting, by all accounts, these were some of the most important and certainly the most controversial decisions.

I also think relatively little attention should be paid to the fact that 42 percent of decisions were unanimous, about the same as in recent years. That is more a reflection of the cases the justices took than it is of a Court where there is any meaningful consensus about the most contentious issues that come before it.

The age of the justices. One final statistic is important for looking ahead to the Court's future. Four justices are over 70: Thomas 77, Alito 75, Sotomayor 71, and Roberts 70. Kagan is 65 and Kavanaugh is 60. The remaining justices are in their 50s: Gorsuch 57, Jackson 54, and Barrett 53.

No justice retired at the end of the term. All are expected to be back for October Term 2025. As discussed in Chapter 14, again the term is likely to be a docket dominated by culture war issues and challenges to President Trump's executive actions. And surely the most important number, this term and next, is 6–3: It is a Court with six conservative justices and three liberal justices. And the bottom line is that it likely will remain a conservative court for many years to come.

The Rhetoric

Not surprisingly, given the matters before the Court, there were occasions of very strongly worded opinions, most notably in the dissents of Justices Sotomayor and Jackson, which are discussed throughout this book. There were a couple of exchanges between justices that were especially sharp and noteworthy that reflected deep underlying disagreements.

Stanley v. City of Sanford involved the ongoing strong disagreement about the proper method of statutory interpretation, with conservative justices professing the need to look only at the plain text, while liberal justices want to focus on identifying and fulfilling the legislature's purpose.[15] The case involved interpreting the federal Americans with Disabilities Act (ADA) and concerned a retired firefighter with Parkinson's disease who sought to sue her former employer under the ADA for canceling her extended health insurance coverage for retirees who left the force before serving 25 years due to a disability. The Court ruled against the firefighter. Justice Gorsuch wrote for the Court and concluded that to prevail under

Title I of the ADA, which prohibits employment discrimination against people with disabilities, a plaintiff must plead and prove that she held or desired a job, and could perform its essential functions with or without reasonable accommodation, at the time of an employer's alleged act of disability-based discrimination.

Justice Gorsuch, who takes a textualist approach to statutory interpretation, accused Justice Jackson of employing an approach to statutory interpretation that was "insufficiently pliable to secure the result" she sought in the case by referencing the statute's "primary purpose" and "legislative history."[16]

Justice Jackson responded directly to this and defended interpreting statutes to fulfill the legislature's purpose. She wrote a strong critique of textualism and defense of purposivism:

> *The majority's contention that I reject "'pure textualism' [a]s insufficiently pliable to secure the result [I] seek," stems from an unfortunate misunderstanding of the judicial role. Our interpretative task is not to seek our own desired results (whatever they may be). And, indeed, it is precisely because of this solemn duty that, in my view, it is imperative that we interpret statutes consistent with all relevant indicia of what Congress wanted, as best we can ascertain its intent. A methodology that includes consideration of Congress's aims does exactly that—and no more. By contrast, pure textualism's refusal to try to understand the text of a statute in the larger context of what Congress sought to achieve turns the interpretive task into a potent weapon for advancing judicial policy preferences. By "finding" answers in ambiguous text, and not bothering to consider whether those answers align with other sources of statutory meaning, pure textualists can easily disguise their own preferences as "textual" inevitabilities. So, really, far from being "insufficiently pliable," I think pure textualism is incessantly malleable—that's its primary problem—and, indeed, it is certainly somehow always flexible enough to secure the majority's desired outcome.*[17]

Another strongly worded disagreement between justices also involved Justice Jackson in the high-profile case of *Trump v. CASA*, in which the Court ended nationwide injunctions.[18] Justice Jackson wrote an impassioned dissent, concluding by stating: "Perhaps the degradation of our rule-of-law regime would happen anyway. But this Court's complicity in the creation of a culture of disdain for lower courts, their rulings, and the law (as they interpret it) will surely hasten the downfall of our governing institutions, enabling our collective demise. . . . Even if '[s]uch institutions may be destined to pass away,' 'it is the duty of the Court to be last, not first, to give them up.'"[19]

Justice Jackson argued that once a court declares an executive practice unconstitutional, it may order the government to follow the law. She wrote: "What I mean by this is that our rights-based legal system can only function properly if the Executive, and everyone else, is *always* bound by law. Today's decision is a seismic shock to that foundational norm. Allowing the Executive to violate the law at its prerogative with respect to anyone who has not yet sued carves out a huge exception—a gash in the basic tenets of our founding charter that could turn out to be a mortal wound."[20]

Justice Barrett, in her majority opinion, responded sharply to Justice Jackson and said: "Justice Jackson, however, chooses a startling line of attack that is tethered neither to these sources nor, frankly, to any doctrine whatsoever. . . . [S]he offers a vision of the judicial role that would make even the most ardent defender of judicial supremacy blush."[21] Justice Barrett continued: "We will not dwell on Justice Jackson's argument, which is at odds with more than two centuries' worth of precedent, not to mention the Constitution itself. We observe only this: Justice Jackson decries an imperial Executive while embracing an imperial Judiciary. . . . Justice Jackson would do well to heed her own admonition: '[E]veryone, from the President on down, is bound by law.' That goes for judges too."[22]

At a time when our country is deeply divided, it is no surprise that a Court with six conservative and three liberal justices is similarly riven.[23] Nor is it a surprise that the justices feel passionately about the important issues before them. This, and the, at times, heated rhetoric, is sure to continue in the years ahead as the justices continue to face divisive issues—as in October Term 2024—that arise from the culture wars and from the actions of a President who repeatedly is testing constitutional limits.

Endnotes

1. Trump v. CASA, Inc., 145 S. Ct. 2540 (2025) (discussed in Chapter 4).

2. *Id.* at 2548.

3. *Id.* at 2565 (quoting Trump v. Hawaii, 138 S. Ct. 2392, 2425 (Thomas, J., concurring)).

4. *Id.* at 2573 (Sotomayor, J., dissenting).

5. *Id.* at 2596–97 (Jackson, J., dissenting).

6. Dep't of Homeland Sec. v. D.V.D., 145 S. Ct. 2627 (2025). In this book, I cover the rulings through June 27, 2025, the last day on which decisions were issued. The Court handed down many additional rulings on its emergency docket over the summer of 2025.

7. Mahmoud v. Taylor, 145 S. Ct. 2332 (2025) (discussed in Chapter 9).

8. United States v. Skrmetti, 145 S. Ct. 1816 (2025).

9. The statistics that follow come from "Statpack" on Scotusblog.com.

10. Dobbs v. Jackson Women's Health Org., 142 S. Ct. 2228 (2022).

11. FCC v. Consumers' Rsch., 145 S. Ct. 2482 (2025) (discussed in Chapter 2).

12. A.L.A. Schechter Poultry v. United States, 55 S. Ct. 837 (1935); Panama Refining Co. v. Ryan, 55 S. Ct. 241 (1935).

13. For an excellent discussion of the Court's emergency docket, *see* STEVEN VLADECK, THE SHADOW DOCKET (2023).

14. Dep't of Homeland Sec. v. D.V.D., 145 S. Ct. 2627 (2025).

15. Stanley v. City of Sanford, 145 S. Ct. 2058 (2025).

16. *Id.* at 2067.

17. *Id.* at 2089 n.12.

18. CASA, 145 S. Ct. at 2540 (2025) (discussed in Chapter 4).

19. *Id.* at 2608 (Jackson, J., dissenting (quoting Youngstown, Sheet & Tube Co. v. Sawyer, 72 S. Ct. 863, 880 (opinion of R. Jackson, J.)).

20. *Id.* at 2602–03.

21. *Id.* at 2560.

22. *Id.* at 2561.

23. *See* ERWIN CHEMERINSKY, A COURT DIVIDED: OCTOBER TERM 2023, at 1–3 (2024) (describing the deep divisions among the justices).

Chapter 2

Administrative Law

In the last few years, the Supreme Court has dramatically changed aspects of federal administrative law. The Court created a new doctrine to limit the power of federal agencies: the major questions doctrine. This is the principle that a federal agency cannot act on a major question of economic or political significance unless it has clear direction from Congress. The Court applied this doctrine to hold that the Environmental Protection Agency lacks authority to regulate greenhouse gas emissions from coal-fired power plants[1] and that the Secretary of Education lacked authority to adopt a loan forgiveness program.[2] This has spawned a great deal of litigation over what is a major question and what is sufficient congressional guidance to allow an agency to act.

A year ago, in a series of October Term 2023 decisions, the Supreme Court significantly changed administrative law, overall reducing the power of federal agencies and increasing the authority of courts over them. In *Loper Bright Enterprises v. Raimondo*, the Court overruled the *Chevron* doctrine, the previously followed principle that courts should defer to reasonable agency interpretations of ambiguous statutes.[3] In *Securities and Exchange Commission v. Jarkesy*, the Court held that agencies cannot impose civil penalties in matters that would have gone to a jury in 1791, concluding that the Seventh Amendment ensures a jury trial in federal court in such cases.[4] And in *Corner Post, Inc. v. Board of Governors of the Federal Reserve System*, the Court extended the time for challenging agency action to six years from when a person is injured, not six years from the time of the agency action.[5]

Each of these developments individually is significant for judges, lawyers, and the law. But cumulatively they are bringing about a dramatic change in the administrative state and the federal government. Each case was a 6–3 decision, with the justices ideologically divided.

The administrative state has been based on the premise that Congress may create federal agencies with broad authority to implement the law, that it is unrealistic for Congress to legislate in great detail and it needs to leave much to the agencies, and that the agencies have expertise that courts should defer to. The liberal justices on the Court continue to accept these premises. But the conservative justices clearly reject them, and their decisions reflect a desire to have more judicial limits and controls over agency powers.

But to use a baseball metaphor, these decisions have been doubles for those who want to dramatically change the administrative state. Their grand slam would be for the Supreme Court to revive the non-delegation doctrine: the principle that Congress cannot delegate its legislative power to executive agencies. If the Court were to invalidate broad delegations of power, virtually every federal agency would be constitutionally vulnerable. The Court had the issue before it in *Federal Communications Commission v. Consumers Research*, but did not strike the federal law down on non-delegation grounds.[6] Also, in *Kennedy v. Braidwood Management Co.*, the Court declined to impose additional restrictions on Congress in determining who can possess the appointment power.[7]

But in a matter on the emergency docket, *Trump v. Wilcox*, the Court strongly indicated a likely major change as to Congress's ability to limit the President's removal power.[8] And in another matter on its emergency docket, in July 2025, the Court further indicated that it supports broad presidential power to fire government employees, notwithstanding protections provided by federal statutes.[9]

The Non-Delegation Doctrine

There is a long-standing principle in American constitutional law that Congress cannot delegate its legislative power, such as to federal agencies.

But only twice in American history has the Court struck down a federal statute on non-delegation grounds. Both cases involved the National Industrial Recovery Act, a key piece of New Deal legislation that authorized the president to approve "codes of fair competition" developed by boards of various industries. In *Panama Refining Co. v. Ryan*, in 1935, the Court declared unconstitutional a provision of the National Industrial Recovery Act that authorized the President to prohibit the shipment in interstate commerce of oil produced in excess of state-imposed production quotas.[10] The Court concluded that the law was an impermissible delegation of legislative power to the President, emphasizing the lack of any standards in the act to limit the President's discretion.

In *Schechter Poultry Corp. v. United States*, also in 1935, the Court declared unconstitutional another regulation adopted under the National Industrial Recovery Act.[11] Pursuant to this law, the President approved a Live Poultry Code for New York City. In part, the Code required sellers to sell only entire coops of chickens or half coops of chickens, and it made it illegal for buyers to reject individual chickens. The Code also regulated employment by requiring collective bargaining, prohibiting child labor, and establishing a 40-hour workweek and a minimum wage. The Court declared that "Congress is not permitted to abdicate or to transfer to others the essential legislative function with which it is thus vested."[12] The Court recognized the need for regulations to deal with the "host of details with which the national legislature cannot deal directly."[13] But the Court said that "the constant recognition of the necessity and validity of such provisions, and the wide range of administrative authority which has been developed by means of them cannot be allowed to obscure the limitations of the authority to delegate, if our constitutional system is to be maintained."[14]

In the 90 years since *Panama Oil* and *Schechter*, not a single federal law has been declared an impermissible delegation of legislative power. Although these decisions have not been expressly overruled, they never have been followed either. All delegations, no matter how broad, have been upheld. Although the Court says that when Congress delegates its legislative power it must provide criteria—"intelligible principles"—to guide the agency's exercise of discretion,[15] all delegations, even without any criteria, have been upheld.

But in 2019, in *Gundy v. United States*, three justices—in a dissenting opinion by Justice Neil Gorsuch and joined by Chief Justice John Roberts and Justice Clarence Thomas—urged the revival of the non-delegation doctrine.[16] Justice Samuel Alito wrote a short opinion concurring in the judgment and said if there were five votes to reconsider the non-delegation doctrine, he would join them.[17] Since then Justices Brett Kavanaugh and Amy Coney Barrett have joined the Court, as has Justice Ketanji Brown Jackson, though she is very unlikely to join the conservatives on this issue.

In *Federal Communications Commission v. Consumers' Research*, the Court had the chance to revive the non-delegation doctrine as a basis for striking down federal laws, but it didn't happen.[18] The case involved provisions of the Telecommunications Act of 1996 that required the Federal Communications Commission (FCC) to facilitate broadband access, including in rural areas and in schools. The law called upon the FCC to create a Universal Service Fund and required every carrier providing interstate telecommunications services to contribute to this. All of our phone bills include a charge for this.

The FCC created the Universal Service Administrative Company as the Fund's "permanent Administrator." It is a private, not-for-profit company. It manages the day-to-day operations of the Fund, "bill[ing] and collect[ing] contributions from carriers" and "distribut[ing] the resulting pot of money, as FCC rules provide, to program beneficiaries."[19] The Company proposes to the FCC what telecommunications companies should contribute. The FCC then decides.

Consumers' Research opposed the amount set in 2021 and challenged the FCC's action in the Court of Appeals for the Fifth Circuit. The Fifth Circuit, in an en banc decision, declared unconstitutional the delegation from Congress to the FCC and the sub-delegation to the Universal Service Administrative Company.[20] The Court of Appeals stressed that it was the combination of the delegation and the sub-delegation that made this unconstitutional.

The Supreme Court, in a 6–3 decision, upheld the federal statute and rejected the non-delegation challenge. Justice Elena Kagan wrote the opinion for the Court. She declared: "We hold that no impermissible transfer of authority has occurred. Under our nondelegation precedents, Congress sufficiently guided and constrained the discretion that it lodged with the FCC to implement the universal-service contribution scheme. And the FCC, in its turn, has retained all decision-making authority within that sphere, relying on the Administrative Company only for non-binding advice. Nothing in those arrangements, either separately or together, violates the Constitution."[21]

As for the claim that Congress had impermissibly delegated power to the FCC, Justice Kagan stressed that the law provides "intelligible principles" to guide the agency in the exercise of its discretion. It is notable that the Court retained and applied this approach to assessing the constitutionality of delegations because it had been criticized, such as in Justice Gorsuch's dissent in *Gundy v. United States.*

The Court expressly rejected the dissent's claim that there is a heightened requirement for specificity when revenue raising is involved.[22] The Court noted that prior decisions had rejected a special limit on delegations involving what might be seen as taxes. Justice Kagan concluded that the law "imposed ascertainable and meaningful guideposts for the FCC to follow when carrying out its delegated function of collecting and spending contributions from carriers."[23] The Court also rejected the argument that there was an impermissible delegation by the FCC to the private company, stressing that the FCC retained control and decision-making authority over every aspect of the fee setting. Having found both the delegation and the sub-delegation to be constitutional, the Court was unpersuaded by the Fifth Circuit's claim that the combination of these made the federal law unconstitutional.

Justice Gorsuch wrote the dissent, joined by Justices Thomas and Alito. The dissent especially focused on the revenue raising aspect of the Universal Service Fund. Justice Gorsuch wrote:

> *The Constitution affords only our elected representatives the power to decide which taxes the government can collect and at what rates. Throughout the Nation's history, Congress has almost invariably respected this assignment. . . . Today, the Court departs from these time-honored rules. When it comes to "universal service" taxes, the Court concludes, an executive agency may decide for itself what rates to apply and how much to collect. In upholding that arrangement, the Court defies the Constitution's command that Congress "may not transfer to another branch 'powers which are strictly and exclusively legislative.'"*[24]

In a sense, this case is the dog that didn't bite this term. The Court did not change the law and it did not revive the non-delegation doctrine. That, of course, could still happen in the future. But Justice Kavanaugh, in a candid concurring opinion, said that the development of the major questions doctrine and the overruling of *Chevron* deference have lessened the concerns with broad delegations of power.[25]

The Appointment Power

Article II, section 2, provides that the President "shall nominate, and by and with the Advice and Consent of the Senate, shall appoint Ambassadors, other public Ministers and Consuls, Judges of the Supreme Court, and all other Officers of the United States, whose Appointments are not herein otherwise provided for, and which shall be established by Law: but the Congress may by Law vest the Appointment of such inferior Officers, as they think proper, in the President alone, to the Courts of Law, or in the Heads of Departments."[26] Under this, the President appoints "officers" of the United States, but Congress has some discretion as to who will appoint "inferior" officers.

In recent cases, the Supreme Court has declared unconstitutional federal statutes on the ground that they had heads of agencies, not the President, appoint "officers" of the United States. For example, in *Lucia v. Securities and Exchange Commission*, the Court held that administrative law judges in the Securities and Exchange Commission should be regarded as "officers" of the United States.[27] The Court noted that they held a "continuing office" and exercised "significant discretion."[28] Similarly, in *United States v. Arthrex, Inc.*, the Court held that Administrative Patent Judges (APJs) were unconstitutionally appointed by the Secretary of Commerce.[29] Chief Justice Roberts wrote the majority opinion and ruled that the powers granted to the APJs via Congress are in violation of the appointments clause. The Court said that an inferior officer must be directed and supervised at some level by leadership appointed by the President and confirmed by the Senate. The majority found it unconstitutional that "Congress ha[d] assigned APJs 'significant authority' in adjudicating the public rights of private parties, while also insulating their decisions from review and their offices from removal."[30]

But this term, in *Kennedy v. Braidwood Management*, the Court rejected such a challenge to the U.S. Preventive Services Task Force, an entity within the Department of Health and Human Services.[31] The Task Force issues public recommendations about preventive healthcare services—for example, cancer and diabetes screenings. Under the Affordable Care Act, health insurers are required to cover some of the recommended services at no cost to the insured.

Members of the Task Force are appointed by the Secretary of Health and Human Services (HSS), not the President. It was argued that this was unconstitutional. But the Supreme Court, in a 6–3 decision in an opinion by Justice Kavanaugh, ruled that the members of the Task Force were "inferior" officers and did not need to be appointed by the President. The Court explained: "The Task Force members are removable at will by the Secretary of HHS, and their recommendations are reviewable by the Secretary before they take effect. So Task Force members are supervised and directed by the Secretary, who in turn answers to the President, preserving the chain of command in Article II. Therefore, under Article II and this Court's precedents, the Task Force members are inferior officers. As a result, appointment of Task Force members by the Secretary of HHS is consistent with the Appointments Clause."[32] Justice Thomas dissented on the grounds that the federal statute did not expressly specify that the members were to be appointed by the Secretary of HHS.[33]

The decision will have practical significance in allowing cabinet officials, such as the Secretary of Health and Human Services, greater power to appointing, and perhaps also to removing, government officials. It also is important because it comes after recent Supreme Court cases that had limited the power of Congress to vest appointment power in other than the President.

The Removal Power

In 1935, in *Humphrey's Executor v. United States*, the Court unanimously upheld the ability of Congress to limit the removal of a commissioner of the Federal Trade Commission.[34] Under the Federal Trade Commission Act, the President could fire a commissioner only for "inefficiency, neglect of duty, or malfeasance in office."[35] The Court explained that Congress, pursuant to its powers under Article I, could create independent agencies and insulate their members from presidential removal unless good cause for firing existed.

Since taking office on January 20, 2025, President Trump has made clear that he does not believe that *Humphrey's Executor* should be regarded as good law and that he will not comply with it.[36] Trump's argument is that it is a "unitary executive," and he should be able to fire anyone in the executive branch of government.

In *Trump v. Wilcox*, a matter on the Supreme Court's emergency docket, the six conservative justices indicated that they are likely to agree with President Trump about this and it suggests the Court is inclined to overrule *Humphrey's Executor.*[37] Gwynne Wilcox was appointed to the National Labor Relations Board by President Joe Biden and confirmed by the Senate. Her term expires in 2028, and federal law provides that she can be fired only for "cause." Cathy Harris is chair of the Merit Systems Protection Board and likewise under the federal statute can be fired only for cause.

President Trump fired both Wilcox and Harris without any assertion of cause for the firing. The district court enjoined the firing and the D.C. Circuit in an en banc decision affirmed.[38] But the Supreme Court in a 6–3 ruling stayed the preliminary injunction, allowing Wilcox and Harris to be fired while the matter was being litigated. In a very short order, the Court said:

> *Because the Constitution vests the executive power in the President, see Art. II, § 1, cl. 1, he may remove without cause executive officers who exercise that power on his behalf, subject to narrow exceptions recognized by our precedents. The stay reflects our judgment that the Government is likely to show that both the NLRB and MSPB exercise considerable executive power. But we do not ultimately decide in this posture whether the NLRB or MSPB falls within such a recognized exception; that question is better left for resolution after full briefing and argument. The stay also reflects our judgment that the Government faces greater risk of harm from an order allowing a removed officer to continue exercising the executive power than a wrongfully removed officer faces from being unable to perform her statutory duty.*[39]

Although the case had nothing to do with the Federal Reserve, the Court went out of its way—perhaps to reassure the stock market—that its holding did apply to that board. The Court explained: "The Federal Reserve is a uniquely structured, quasi-private entity that follows in the distinct historical tradition of the First and Second Banks of the United States."[40]

Justice Kagan wrote a strong dissent, joined by Justices Sotomayor and Jackson. She defended *Humphrey's Executor*, stating the decision "undergirds a significant feature of American governance: bipartisan administrative bodies carrying out expertise-based functions with a measure of independence from presidential control."[41] She said that under *Humphrey's Executor*, the firings were clearly illegal. She wrote that "the order allows the President to overrule *Humphrey's* by fiat, again pending our eventual review."[42] She strongly objected to the Court seeming to change the law on its "shadow docket" without the benefit of briefing and oral argument.

The bottom line is that the Court did not overrule *Humphrey's Executor*, but gave a strong signal that it is likely to do so.

Subsequently, in another matter on the Supreme Court's emergency docket, the Court appeared to grant the President broad power to fire government employees. *Trump v. American Federation of Government Employees* involved a federal district court order that enjoined the President from engaging in massive reductions in force in federal agencies.[43] The Court found large-scale layoffs and reorganizations across several federal agencies, including the Departments of Agriculture, Health and Human Services, and State, exceeded presidential authority in ordering these reductions without congressional approval. The U.S. Court of Appeals for the Ninth Circuit denied the United States government a stay of the district court's preliminary injunction.

But the Supreme Court issued a stay and briefly stated: "Because the Government is likely to succeed on its argument that the Executive Order and Memorandum are lawful—and because the other factors bearing on whether to grant a stay are satisfied—we grant the application. We express no view on the legality of any Agency RIF and Reorganization Plan produced or approved pursuant to the Executive Order and Memorandum."[44]

Only Justice Jackson dissented. She objected that the Court was "allow[ing] an apparently unprecedented and congressionally unsanctioned dismantling of the Federal Government to continue apace, causing irreparable harm before courts can determine whether the President has the authority to engage in the actions he proposes."[45]

These, of course, are rulings on the emergency docket, not decisions on the merits. But the Court's conclusion that the President is likely to succeed in both cases on the merits indicates that a majority of the justices are likely to go very far in according the President the power to fire anyone in the executive branch of government. This may mean not only the power to fire heads of agencies, but even that protections under civil service law may be declared unconstitutional.

Conclusion

October Term 2024, unlike recent terms, did not see the Court imposing significant new limits on administrative agencies. But the issues are sure to return, and this term seems more like a pause than a shift in direction. And the matters on the emergency docket indicate a Court likely poised to significantly change the law with regard to the ability of Congress to limit the President's removal power.

Endnotes

1. West Virginia v. EPA, 142 S. Ct. 2587 (2022) (holding that the Environmental Protection Agency lacked the authority to regulate greenhouse gas emissions from coal fired power plants).
2. Biden v. Nebraska, 143 S. Ct. 2355 (2023) (holding that the Biden administration lacked the authority to provide student loan relief).
3. Loper Bright Enters. v. Raimondo, 144 S. Ct. 2244 (2024).
4. SEC v. Jarkesy, 144 S. Ct. 2117 (2024).
5. Corner Post, Inc. v. Bd. of Governors of the Fed. Rsrv. Sys., 144 S. Ct. 2440 (2024).
6. FCC v. Consumers' Rsch., 145 S. Ct. 587 (2024).
7. Kennedy v. Braidwood Mgmt., 145 S. Ct. 2427 (2025).
8. Trump v. Wilcox, 145 S. Ct. 1415 (2025).
9. Trump v. Nat'l Fed'n of Gov't Emps., 145 S. Ct. 2635 (2025).
10. Panama Refining Co. v. Ryan, 293 U.S. 388 (1935).
11. A.L.A. Schechter Poultry Corp. v. United States, 295 U.S. 495 (1935).

12. *Id.* at 529.
13. *Id.* at 530.
14. *Id.*
15. *See, e.g.*, Whitman v. Am. Trucking Ass'ns, Inc., 531 U.S. 457 (2001); Nat'l Cable Television Ass'n v. United States, 415 U.S. 336 (1974).
16. Gundy v. United States, 139 S. Ct. 2116, 2130 (2019) (Gorsuch, J., dissenting).
17. *Id.* at 2131 (Alito, J., concurring).
18. FCC v. Consumers' Rsch., 145 S. Ct. 2482 (2025).
19. *Id.* at 2495 (citations omitted).
20. Consumers' Rsch. v. FCC, 109 F.4th 743 (5th Cir. 2024) (en banc).
21. FCC v. Consumers' Rsch. at 2497.
22. *Id.* at 2495.
23. *Id.* at 2501.
24. *Id.* at 2519.
25. *Id.* at 2511 (Kavanaugh, J., concurring).
26. U.S. Const. art. II, § 2.
27. Lucia v. SEC, 138 S. Ct. 2044 (2018).
28. *Id.* at 2053.
29. United States v. Arthrex, Inc., 141 S. Ct. 1970 (2021).
30. *Id.* at 1986.
31. Kennedy v. Braidwood Mgmt., 145 S. Ct. 2427 (2025).
32. *Id.* at 2439.
33. *Id.* at 2461 (Thomas, J., dissenting).
34. Humphrey's Ex'r v. United States, 295 U.S. 602 (1935).
35. 15 U.S.C. § 41.
36. Letter from Susan Harris, Acting Solicitor General, to Rep. J. Raskin, Re: Restrictions on the Removal of Certain Principal Officers of the United States (Feb. 12, 2025).
37. Trump v. Wilcox, 145 S. Ct. 1415 (2025).
38. Wilcox v. Trump, 775 F. Supp. 3d 215 (D.C. Cir. 2025).
39. Trump v. Wilcox, 145 S. Ct. at 1416.
40. *Id.* at 1417.
41. *Id.* (Kagan, J., dissenting).
42. *Id.* at 1419 (Kagan, J., dissenting).
43. 145 S. Ct. 2635 (2025).
44. *Id.*
45. *Id.* at 2635–36 (Jackson, J., dissenting).

Chapter 3

Business Law Cases

There were several important cases concerning business law that arose under federal statutes. The Court considered cases regarding the False Claims Act, the Lanham Act protecting against trademark infringement, the Bankruptcy Act, and the civil RICO statute.

False Claims Act

The False Claims Act, a law enacted in 1863, allows suits by both the government and individuals suing on behalf of the U.S. government to recover funds lost due to fraud against the government.[1] It targets those who knowingly submit false claims for payment to the government, use false records to get a claim paid, or avoid obligations to pay the government. Defendants can be ordered to pay treble damages, as well as other penalties.

In *Wisconsin Bell v. United States*,[2] the Supreme Court considered what is a "claim" for purposes of the False Claims Act in a case arising under the Telecommunications Act of 1996. Under that law, telecommunications carriers are required to deposit certain amounts into a central fund, the Universal Service Fund.[3] This money is distributed via the Education-Rate (E-Rate) program, which subsidizes telecommunications services for schools and libraries.

Todd Heath, an auditor of telecommunications bills, brought suit against Wisconsin Bell under the False Claims Act, claiming Wisconsin Bell had violated the "lowest corresponding price" rule, submitted inflated reimbursements requests, and defrauded the E-Rate program out of millions of dollars.

To be considered a "claim" under the False Claims Act, the government needs to have "provided any portion of the money requested."[4] Wisconsin Bell contended that this requirement was not met because all the money in the Universal Service Fund comes from private carriers, and a private carrier handles its collection and disbursement. Thus, the argument was that the E-Rate program is "private," and the government does not provide any portion of the money.

The issue in this case was therefore whether an E-Rate reimbursement request qualifies as a "claim" under the False Claims Act. Both the district court and the Seventh Circuit found the FCA definition of "claim" was met, pointing to the high degree of government involvement in facilitating funds.[5]

In a unanimous decision, with Justice Elena Kagan writing the majority opinion, the Supreme Court affirmed and found that E-Rate reimbursement requests qualify as FCA "claims." Justice Kagan pointed to the over $100 million deposited "directly from the U.S. Treasury" into the Universal Service Fund to establish the government's provision. Rather than acting as a "passive throughway" for E-Rate, "[t]he Government supplied funds, furnished funds, and made available funds for that purpose. It is a simple matter, as the saying goes, of following the money."[6]

The case is important as to the ability to bring False Claims Act suits under the Telecommunications Act and, more generally, in clarifying that the involvement of government funds can be a basis for suits under the False Claims Act. But the larger long-term significance of the case might be in a one paragraph concurring opinion by Justice Brett Kavanaugh, joined by Justice Clarence Thomas.[7] Justice Kavanaugh wrote: "I join the Court's opinion, which decides a narrow statutory question regarding the scope of the False Claims Act. That statutory issue arises in the context of a *qui tam* suit. The Act's *qui tam* provisions raise substantial constitutional questions under Article II. Those constitutional questions are not before the Court in this case. But in an appropriate case, the Court should consider the competing arguments on the Article II issue."[8]

The argument, which these justices have raised before,[9] is that the False Claims Act is unconstitutional in authorizing individuals to bring suits on behalf of the federal government. Their argument is that only the executive branch of government, under the control of the President, can decide whether to sue for the federal government. These suits, referred to as qui tam actions, have existed since the False Claims Act was adopted in 1863. It would be a dramatic change in the law to declare this unconstitutional and for the Court to hold that Congress cannot authorize suits on behalf of the United States government. One lower federal court already has come to that conclusion, so the issue is sure to return to the Supreme Court.[10] It is unclear whether the Court's majority will agree with Justices Kavanaugh and Thomas, but as discussed in Chapter 2, it appears that a majority of the justices agree with the premise of the argument that it is a "unitary executive" under the control of the President.

Damages for Trademark Infringements

In *Dewberry Group, Inc. v. Dewberry Engineers*, the issue was how to determine the award of profits for purposes of awarding damages in a trademark infringement case.[11] Dewberry Engineers, a commercial real estate development services provider, owns a registered trademark in the word "Dewberry." Dewberry Group, another unrelated commercial real estate company, provides services to a portfolio of about 30 affiliate companies. A 2007 trademark infringement suit brought by the Dewberry Engineers resulted in a settlement that the Dewberry Group limit its use of the word "Dewberry." But about a decade later, the Dewberry Group reneged on the deal and resumed its use of the "Dewberry" name as part of a rebranding effort.

Dewberry Engineers sued again, and the district court found Dewberry Group liable for trademark infringement. Under section 1117(a) of the Lanham Act, a prevailing plaintiff may recover the "defendant's profits" deriving from a trademark violation. The court granted Dewberry Engineers a $43 million award, a number that calculated the Dewberry Group and its 30 affiliates as a single corporate entity. The Dewberry Group objected, contending that its affiliates do not constitute a part of the "defendant's profits."

The Fourth Circuit affirmed the award, reiterating the "economic reality" of Dewberry Group's relationship with its affiliates meant ruling otherwise would give businesses a "blueprint for using corporate formalities to insulate their infringement from financial consequences."[12] But the Supreme Court vacated and remanded the case, finding the lower courts erred in treating Dewberry Group and its affiliates as a single entity. The Court, in an opinion by Justice Kagan, found that treating affiliates as a single entity disregards "corporate formalities" and the "principle of corporate separateness."[13] Even if entities are affiliated or have a common owner, "it is long settled as a matter of American corporate law that separately incorporated organizations are separate legal units with distinct legal rights and obligations."[14] Thus, Dewberry Group was the sole defendant and only its own profits were recoverable.

Justice Sonia Sotomayor wrote separately to underscore that principles of corporate separateness "do not force courts to close their eyes to practical realities" in calculating a "defendant's profits."[15] Justice Sotomayor references the Lanham Act's directive that courts calculate profits "subject to the principles of equity." Under those principles, companies cannot evade accountability for wrongdoing through creative accounting, "including efforts to obscure a defendant's true financial gain through arrangements with affiliates."[16] Justice Sotomayor suggests that upon remand the lower courts explore the issue and consider reopening the record if appropriate.

Bankruptcy Law

In *Central Virginia Community College v. Katz*, the Supreme Court held that the Bankruptcy Act abrogated states' sovereign immunity, concluding that was part of "the plan of the Constitutional Convention."[17] In *United States v. Miller*, the Supreme Court returned to the issue of sovereign immunity in the bankruptcy context in construing the scope of the sovereign immunity waiver in the bankruptcy law.[18]

A Utah-based business fell into insolvency in 2013, filing for bankruptcy three years later. The appointed trustee of the bankruptcy state filed suit against the government under section 544(b) of the Bankruptcy Code, seeking to avoid tax payments made in 2014 during a time of insolvency.

The Bankruptcy Code contains a sovereign-immunity waiver that abrogates the government's sovereign immunity "with respect to" section 544. To show that a transfer is "voidable under applicable law," section 544(b) requires a trustee to identify an actual creditor capable of voiding the transfer at issue under "applicable law." The trustee invoked Utah's fraudulent-transfer statute as the source of "applicable law" for his claim.

This case involves the bankruptcy trustee's avoidance powers under section 544(b), and whether the scope of section 106(a)'s waiver also abrogates sovereign immunity with respect to the underlying state law claim that supplies the "applicable law" for a trustee's section 544(b) claim. The bankruptcy court and district court found section 106(a) waived the government's sovereign immunity. The Tenth Circuit affirmed, concluding that section 106(a) "expresses Congress's intent to abolish the Government's sovereign immunity in an avoidance proceeding arising under § 544(b)(1), regardless of the context in which the defense arises."[19]

The Supreme Court, in a 7–1 decision, reversed, finding section 106(a)'s sovereign-immunity waiver applies only to the section 544(b) claim itself and not to any state law claims nested within that federal claim. Justice Jackson delivered the opinion of the Court, finding that waivers of sovereign immunity must be narrowly read because "[u]nder long-settled law, Congress must use unmistakable language to abrogate sovereign immunity."[20] The Court concluded: "Section 106(a) of the Bankruptcy Code abrogates sovereign immunity for the federal cause of action created by § 544(b). It does not take the additional step of abrogating sovereign immunity for whatever state-law claim supplies the 'applicable law' for a trustee's § 544(b) claim."[21]

Justice Gorsuch wrote a dissenting opinion, finding section 106(a)(1) bars the government from raising the affirmative defense of sovereign immunity. He wrote:

> *It seems to me, however, that the Court conflates two different things. Whether pursued by a private creditor or a bankruptcy trustee, a good substantive claim for relief exists. No one disputes that a fraudulent transfer took place. The question before us is a distinct one: Can the federal government defeat the claim by raising the affirmative defense of sovereign*

> *immunity? With respect to a private creditor pursuing relief in state court, the answer is yes. With respect to a trustee pursuing relief in a federal bankruptcy proceeding, the answer—thanks to § 106(a)(1)—is no.*[22]

One interesting aspect of this disagreement is that historically it has been the liberal justices who have sought to limit sovereign immunity and the conservative justices who have championed it.[23] In this case, it was the liberal justices who found sovereign immunity barred the suit, while the conservative justices dissented from that holding.

Civil RICO Suits

Medical Marijuana, Inc. sells Dixie X, a product that advertises itself as a "CBD-rich, non-psychoactive medicine" that is "0% THC" and legal to use in the U.S. To alleviate chronic pain and reliant upon this information, Douglas Horn began using Dixie X. A few weeks later, upon a random drug screening at his place of work, THC was detected in Horn's system, and he was fired.

Horn brought suit against Medical Marijuana under Racketeer Influence and Corrupt Organizations Act's (RICO) private right of action, alleging Medical Marijuana's false advertising constituted mail and wire fraud. To establish a civil RICO violation under section 1964(c), a plaintiff must show the defendant engaged in a "pattern of racketeering activity" that caused the plaintiff to be "injured in his business or property."[24] Horn argued he had suffered such a business injury in the form of his lost employment. Medical Marijuana objected, contending civil RICO categorically excludes personal injury, which was what was suffered by Horn in this case.

The issue in *Medical Marijuana, Inc. v. Horn* is whether civil RICO denies a remedy for business or property loss that derives from a personal injury, imposing what was called an "antecedent-personal-injury bar."[25] The antecedent-personal-injury bar is a rule that was adopted by several circuits that precludes recovery for business or property losses that derive from a personal injury. Simply put, does the bar on recovery for personal injuries under civil RICO apply even when they result in business or property losses?

The federal district court granted Medical Marijuana summary judgment, finding that because Horn could not recover for a personal injury under RICO's civil cause of action, he could not recover for business or property harm resulting from a personal injury. Upon appeal, the Second Circuit reversed, holding that section 1964(c) does not impose an antecedent-personal-injury bar. Deepening a circuit split, the Second Circuit held that civil RICO permits a plaintiff to sue for injuries to business or property that "flow from, or are derivative of, an antecedent personal injury."[26] In other words, the court concluded that civil RICO does not preclude recovery for personal injuries that are tied to business or property losses.

In a 5–4 decision, the Supreme Court affirmed the Second Circuit's rejection of the antecedent-personal-injury bar. Justice Amy Coney Barrett wrote the opinion for the Court, and was joined by Justices Sotomayor, Kagan, and Jackson. The civil RICO statute allows RICOs to create a civil cause of action only to a "person injured in his *business* or *property*."[27] The Court held that a plaintiff could seek damages for business or property loss under civil-action provision of RICO regardless of whether the loss resulted from personal injury. Justice Barrett concluded: "The phrase 'injured in his business or property' does not preclude recovery for all economic harms that result from personal injuries."[28]

Justice Jackson filed a concurring opinion to offer additional support to the majority's conclusion, citing Congress's directive that RICO "shall be liberally construed to effectuate its remedial purposes."[29]

Justice Thomas delivered a dissenting opinion, establishing he would have dismissed certiorari because the case assumes the existence of a personal injury in the first place, "[y]et, in this case, the parties vigorously contest whether Horn suffered a personal injury at all."[30] Given this lack of clarity, Justice Thomas found this case was an improper vehicle for the question at hand.

Justice Kavanaugh wrote a lengthy dissent, joined by Chief Justice Roberts and Justice Alito, urging "[a] plaintiff cannot circumvent RICO's categorical exclusion of personal-injury suits simply by converting otherwise excluded personal-injury suits into business- or property-injury suits."[31] Justice Kavanaugh predicted negative implications to the majority's decision, stating "the aftermath of the Court's opinion could be quite a mess, as courts grapple with RICO personal-injury cases where the question is what losses qualify as business or property losses."[32] This was one of only two cases all term where Chief Justice Roberts was in dissent.

The case is important in narrowing the preclusion of recovery under civil RICO for personal injuries. Plaintiffs can recover for them if they are tied to losses in business or property.

Endnotes

1. 31 U.S.C. § 3729(b)(2)(A)(ii).
2. Wis. Bell v. United States, 145 S. Ct. 498 (2025).
3. The Universal Service Fund, and its constitutionality, was at issue in *Fed. Commc'ns Comm'n v. Consumers Rsch.*, 145 S. Ct. 2482 (2025). This case, which upheld the constitutionality of the Universal Service Fund, is discussed in Chapter 2.
4. 31 U.S.C. § 3729.
5. United States v. Wis. Bell, 593 F. Supp. 3d 855 (E.D. Wis. 2022); United States v. Wis. Bell, 92 F.4th 654, 666, 667, 669, 671 (7th Cir.).
6. *Id.* at 504, 506–07.
7. 145 S. Ct. at 515 (Kavanaugh, J. concurring).
8. *Id.*
9. *See, e.g.*, *United States ex rel.* Polansky v. Exec. Health Res., Inc., 599 U.S. 419, 442 (2023) (Kavanaugh, J., concurring); *id.* at 449–52 (Thomas, J., dissenting).
10. United States *ex rel.* Zafirov v. Fla. Med. Assocs., LLC, 751 F. Supp. 3d 1293 (M.D. Fla. 2024).
11. Dewberry Grp., Inc. v. Dewberry Eng'rs, 145 S. Ct. 681 (2025).
12. *Id.* at 686.
13. *Id.* at 687.
14. *Id.* at 686.
15. *Id.* at 690 (Sotomayor, J., concurring).
16. *Id.* at 689–90.
17. *See, e.g.*, Cent. Va. Cmty. Coll. v. Katz, 546 U.S. 356 (2006) (holding that the Bankruptcy Act abrogated sovereign immunity).
18. United States v. Miller, 145 S. Ct. 839 (2025).
19. Miller v. United States, 71 F.4th 1247, 1253 (10th Cir. 2023).
20. 145 S. Ct. at 852.
21. *Id.* at 856.
22. *Id.* at 857 (Gorsuch, J., dissenting).

23. *See* ERWIN CHEMERINSKY, FEDERAL JURISDICTION 403–08 (9th ed. 2025).
24. 18 U.S.C. § 1964(c).
25. 145 S. Ct. 931, 937–38 (2025).
26. Horn v. Med. Marijuana, Inc., 80 F.4th 130, 135 (2d Cir. 2023).
27. 145 S. Ct. at 938.
28. *Id.* at 946.
29. *Id.* (Jackson, J., concurring).
30. *Id.* at 948 (Thomas J., dissenting).
31. *Id.* at 953 (Kavanaugh, J., dissenting).
32. *Id.*

Chapter 4

Civil Procedure and Federal Jurisdiction

No case this term received more attention or may be more important in the long term than *Trump v. CASA, Inc.*, which limited the power of federal courts to issue nationwide injunctions.[1] There also were decisions about standing, personal jurisdiction, and removal jurisdiction.[2]

Trump v. CASA, Inc.

On January 20, 2025, President Donald Trump issued an executive order that aimed to limit birthright citizenship in the United States.[3] Three federal district courts ruled that the chief executive's act was unconstitutional and subsequently issued nationwide injunctions. The Supreme Court granted review to decide whether federal courts had the authority to issue such universal injunctions. The question presented was "whether the Supreme Court should stay the district courts' preliminary injunctions except as to the individual plaintiffs and identified members of the organizational plaintiffs or states." Although the Court did not grant review on or decide the constitutionality of the restriction on birthright citizenship, the underlying issue involves one of President Trump's most controversial executive orders.

In *Dred Scott v. Sanford*, in 1857, the Supreme Court held that enslaved individuals were not United States citizens even if they were born in the United States.[4] The first sentence of the 14th Amendment was meant to expressly overrule this holding and states: "All persons born or naturalized in the United States, and subject to the jurisdiction thereof, are citizens of the United States and of the State wherein they reside."

In *United States v. Wong Kim Ark*, in 1898, the Supreme Court interpreted this provision to mean that everyone born in the United States, regardless of the immigration status or citizenship of their parents, is a United States citizen.[5] The Court came to this conclusion by reviewing English law and early American law concerning this and declared: "That all children, born within the dominion of the United States, of foreign parents holding no diplomatic office, became citizens at the time of their birth, does not appear to have been contested or doubted until more than 50 years after the adoption of the constitution."[6] In a 6–2 decision, which carefully reviewed the history of this provision of the 14th Amendment, the Court held that all born in the United States, with very limited exceptions, are citizens of the United States.

The constitutional issue as to the Trump executive order and ultimately the case before the Supreme Court is what the phrase "subject to the jurisdiction thereof" means. The Court expressly addressed that in *Wong Kim Ark* and concluded that it excluded only "children born of alien enemies in hostile occupation, and children of diplomatic representatives of a foreign state." All others born in the United States are American citizens. That has been the understanding of the clause for over a century.

But on January 20, President Trump issued an executive order that states that the 14th Amendment does not bestow citizenship on children whose parents are not lawfully in the United States. Specifically, the executive order provides that individuals born in the United States are not citizens either "when that person's mother was unlawfully present in the United States and the father was not a United States citizen or lawful permanent resident at the time of said person's birth," or "when that person's mother's presence in the United States at the time of said person's birth was lawful but temporary . . . and the father was not a United States citizen or lawful permanent resident at the time of said person's birth."[7] Simply stated, after February 19, only those born to parents who are citizens or green card holders are United States citizens.

Lawsuits immediately were filed challenging President Trump's executive order. Four federal district courts found the birthright citizenship executive order to be unconstitutional and issued nationwide injunctions. Their rulings were upheld in federal courts of appeals. The Trump administration sought Supreme Court review in three cases: *Trump v. CASA*, *Trump v. Washington*, and *Trump v. New Jersey*.

The Trump administration's petition for Supreme Court review said that it was making a "modest" request, arguing that the Court should limit injunctions "to the individual plaintiffs and the identified members of the organizational plaintiffs."[8] The Solicitor General's brief further argued that nationwide injunctions are unconstitutional and that a federal court's power to grant relief is limited to the parties in the lawsuit.

The Supreme Court, in a 6–3 decision, held that federal courts generally cannot issue nationwide injunctions. The Court's decision was based entirely on how it interpreted statutes providing for federal jurisdiction; it did not rule on the constitutionality of nationwide injunctions as the Solicitor General had urged. Justice Amy Coney Barrett wrote for the Court, with Justices Thomas, Alito, and Kavanaugh writing concurring opinions. Justices Sotomayor and Jackson each wrote scathing dissents. Justice Kagan joined Justice Sotomayor's dissent.

Justice Barrett's majority opinion began by declaring: "A universal injunction can be justified only as an exercise of equitable authority, yet Congress has granted federal courts no such power."[9] She said that the inquiry is historical: "We must therefore ask whether universal injunctions are sufficiently 'analogous' to the relief issued 'by the High Court of Chancery in England at the time of the adoption of the Constitution and the enactment of the original Judiciary Act.'"[10]

She answered her question by declaring: "The answer is no: Neither the universal injunction nor any analogous form of relief was available in the High Court of Chancery in England at the time of the founding."[11] She says that nationwide injunctions did not begin until 1963 and were unusual until recent years.[12]

The Court dismissed the relevance of the policy arguments in favor of nationwide injunctions. Justice Barrett wrote: "But as with most questions of law, the policy pros and cons are beside the point. Under our well-established precedent, the equitable relief available in the federal courts are those 'traditionally accorded by courts of equity' at the time of our founding. Nothing like a universal injunction was available at the founding, or for that matter, for more than a century thereafter. Thus, under the Judiciary Act, federal courts lack authority to issue them."[13] The Court explained that a federal court cannot provide greater relief than the relief necessary to remedy for the named plaintiffs in a lawsuit.

The Court's decision recognized that federal courts might be able to provide broad relief via class action suits pursuant to Federal Rule of Civil Procedure 23(b)(2) and also by state governments suing to protect their residents. But the Court did not elaborate on either of these or whether the requirements are likely to be met, expressly saying that the latter was an open question as to whether states have standing to bring such litigation. Nor did the Court rule on whether a federal court can vacate an agency action, effectively nullifying it for the country. In a footnote, Justice Barrett stated: "Nothing we say today resolves the distinct question whether the Administrative Procedure Act authorizes federal courts to vacate federal agency action. See 5 U.S.C. § 706(2) (authorizing courts to "hold unlawful and set aside agency action").[14]

Justice Clarence Thomas, in a concurring opinion, explained the impact of the decision: "The Court today puts an end to the 'increasingly common' practice of federal courts issuing universal injunctions."[15] Both he and Justice Alito, who wrote a separate concurring opinion, urged district courts to be restrained in allowing nationwide relief through class action suits. Justice Samuel Alito concluded his concurring opinion: "But district courts should not view today's decision as an invitation to certify nationwide classes without scrupulous adherence to the rigors of Rule 23. Otherwise, the universal injunction will return from the grave under the guise of 'nationwide class relief,' and today's decision will be of little more than minor academic interest."[16]

Justice Brett Kavanaugh wrote a concurring opinion that took a different approach. He said that the issue of nationwide injunctions is really a matter of timing: What happens between when a district court declared a federal action unconstitutional and when it comes to the Supreme Court? A nationwide injunction stops the practice in the entire country until the Supreme Court hears the matter. Without a nationwide injunction, the government's action can typically continue in the areas where it has not been restrained until the Supreme Court rules. Justice Kavanaugh said that the solution is to bring the matters to the Supreme Court on its emergency docket. He wrote: "When a stay or injunction application arrives here, this Court should not and cannot hide in the tall grass. When we receive such an application, we must grant or deny. And when we do—that is, when this Court makes a decision on the interim legal status of a major new federal statute or executive action—that decision will often constitute a form of precedent (de jure or de facto) that provides guidance throughout the United States during the years-long interim period until a final decision on the merits."[17] Justice Kavanaugh said that the Supreme Court is open 365 days a year, 24 hours a day, and is available to decide the constitutional questions, making nationwide injunctions unnecessary.

Both Justice Sotomayor and Justice Jackson wrote vehement dissents, as strong as any to be found in the United States Reports. Both saw this case in apocalyptic terms, fearing that the Supreme Court was lessening the ability of courts to restrain unconstitutional presidential actions. Justice Sotomayor wrote: "No right is safe in the new legal regime the Court creates. Today, the threat is to birthright citizenship. Tomorrow, a different administration may try to seize firearms from law-abiding citizens or prevent people of certain faiths from gathering to worship. The majority holds that, absent cumbersome class-action litigation, courts cannot completely enjoin even such plainly unlawful policies unless doing so is necessary to afford the formal parties complete relief. That holding renders constitutional guarantees meaningful in name only for any individuals who are not parties to a lawsuit. Because I will not be complicit in so grave an attack on our system of law, I dissent."[18] Likewise, Justice Jackson lamented in her dissent, "The Court's decision to permit the Executive to violate the Constitution with respect to anyone who has not yet sued is an existential threat to the rule of law."[19]

The two dissenting opinions took different approaches. Justice Sotomayor disagreed with every aspect of the majority opinion. Alone among the opinions in the case, she focused on President Trump's executive order limiting birthright citizenship and its unconstitutionality.

Justice Sotomayor also argued that at common law, courts could issue nationwide relief and that equity always gave federal courts authority to fashion necessary remedies to provide complete redress. She said that nationwide injunctions are not new and have existed for over a century. Most of all, she objected that the Court's decision was making it harder for the judiciary to restrain unconstitutional presidential actions. She wrote: "The Court's decision is nothing less than an open invitation for the Government to bypass the Constitution. The Executive Branch can now enforce policies that flout settled law and violate countless individuals' constitutional rights, and the federal courts will be hamstrung to stop its actions fully. Until the day that every affected person manages to become party to a lawsuit and secures for himself injunctive relief, the Government may act lawlessly indefinitely."[20]

Justice Jackson, too, expressed this, but she disagreed with the majority on another ground. She argued that once a federal court declares a presidential action or federal law unconstitutional, it should be deemed invalid until and unless that decision is overruled. Like Justice Sotomayor, she saw grave implications from the Court's decision:

> *Make no mistake: Today's ruling allows the Executive to deny people rights that the Founders plainly wrote into our Constitution, so long as those individuals have not found a lawyer or asked a court in a particular manner to have their rights protected. This perverse burden shifting cannot coexist with the rule of law. In essence, the Court has now shoved lower court judges out of the way in cases where executive action is challenged, and has gifted the Executive with the prerogative of sometimes disregarding the law. As a result, the Judiciary—the one institution that is solely responsible for ensuring our Republic endures as a Nation of laws—has put both our legal system, and our system of government, in grave jeopardy.*[21]

There obviously was profound disagreement between the majority and the dissent. First, they disagreed over methodology and how the Court should go about answering the question of whether federal courts can issue nationwide injunctions. The majority says that the answer is entirely based on history and whether this power, or one closely analogous to it, existed in the High Court of Chancery in England when the Constitution and the Judiciary Act of 1789 were written.

The dissent disagrees with this approach and whether the power of federal courts to restrain the President today should be determined by what the High Court of Chancery in England could do. Justice Jackson says that courts in England lacked the power to restrain the king, so looking to their authority is misguided: "So, it makes little sense to look to the relationship between English courts and the King for guidance on the power of our Nation's Judiciary vis-à-vis its Executive."[22]

Second, the majority and the dissent disagree over what history reveals with regard to the power of federal courts to issue nationwide injunctions. The Court says that universal injunctions did not occur until after the middle of the 20th century, which further reveals their impermissibility. Justice Sotomayor in her dissent argued that at English common law there was a "bill of peace," which was analogous to a nationwide injunction. The Court, though, disagrees and sees a bill of peace as instead like a modern class action. Justice Sotomayor contended that nationwide injunctions are not new and have existed for over a century, but more importantly that historically courts exercising equitable powers always have had broad discretion in fashioning remedies.

Third, the majority and the dissent disagree sharply over the need for nationwide injunctions to check the President. Justice Barrett's majority opinion is highly formalistic and expressly eschews any consideration of policy arguments for nationwide injunctions or the context of the need to check a President who is acting unconstitutionally. For the dissent, this case is all about the need for judicial power to stop unconstitutional presidential actions, now and in the future. The dissent also was concerned about the practical implications of ending nationwide injunctions. The dissenting justices expressed concern that the Court's decision will mean that a challenge to an unconstitutional government policy would have to be brought separately in each of the 94 federal district courts and ultimately in every federal circuit. The dissenters feared that the ruling will mean that when a federal district court finds an executive action unconstitutional, the President can continue to follow it in every other place where it has not yet been declared unconstitutional.

The crucial question going forward is whether alternatives—class action suits pursuant to Rule 23 of the Federal Rules of Civil Procedure, suits by state governments, and vacating agency actions under the Administrative Procedures Act—can achieve the goals of nationwide injunctions in stopping unconstitutional presidential actions or federal statutes for the entire country. The Court leaves these paths possible, though it is unclear whether and when they can be used. Justices Thomas and Alito each wrote concurring opinions urging a narrow approach to courts using these mechanisms.

Ultimately, the availability of these mechanisms will be crucial in determining the practical consequences of the decision. At a time when there is a President who is pushing constitutional boundaries in countless actions, what will it mean for the Supreme Court to have made it much harder for courts to restrain the President?

Standing

It is well established that in order for a plaintiff to have standing to sue in federal court there must be injury, causation, and redressability.[23] In *Diamond Alternative Energy, LLC v. Environmental Protection Agency*, the Supreme Court found that fossil fuel producers had standing to challenge the Environmental Protection Agency's (EPA) allowing California to adopt laws requiring a shift in the state to electric vehicles and away from gas-powered vehicles.[24] As the Court explained, their rationale was that "without California's regulations in effect, manufacturers would likely make more cars powered by gasoline and other liquid fuels, thereby increasing purchases of those fuels and redressing the fuel producers' injury."[25] The EPA and California argued that there was no standing because the fuel producers' injury would not be redressed by a favorable court decision: "Even if the regulations are invalidated, car manufacturers nonetheless would not manufacture more gasoline-powered cars."[26]

In a 7–2 decision written by Justice Brett Kavanaugh—with dissents by Justices Sotomayor and Jackson—the Court found there was standing.

Justice Kavanaugh stressed the relationship between causation and redressability: When the defendant is the cause of the plaintiff's injuries, stopping the defendant's conduct is likely to redress the harms. The Court said that was the case here:

> *In this case, those commonsense economic principles support the fuel producers' standing. The California regulations force automakers to manufacture more electric vehicles and fewer gasoline-powered vehicles. The standards force automakers to produce a fleet of vehicles that, as a whole, uses significantly less gasoline and other liquid fuels. California's regulation of automakers' vehicle fleets in turn will likely 'cause downstream or upstream economic injuries to others in the chain,' such as producers of gasoline and other liquid fuels. By the same token, the fuel producers persuasively contend that invalidating California's regulations would likely mean more gasoline-powered automobiles, which would in turn likely mean more sales of gasoline and other liquid fuels by the fuel producers.*[27]

Two things are particularly interesting about the case. First, the Court ruled on it even though it was likely that the Trump administration was about to change the EPA waiver for California, as it did during the first Trump term. This would render the issue moot.

Second, Justice Jackson wrote a forceful dissent arguing that the Court uses a different and more favorable standard for standing when the plaintiff is a corporation as opposed to an impoverished individual or a civil rights organization. She wrote: "The Court's substantive Article III standing analysis, though not entirely implausible, also invites questions about inconsistent decisionmaking and whether this Court is holding business litigants to the same standards as everyone else. The majority has made nothing short of a herculean effort to justify the conclusion that redressability exists on this record."[28] She lamented: "The Constitution does not distinguish between plaintiffs whose claims are backed by the Chamber of Commerce and those who seek to vindicate their rights to fair housing, desegregated schools, or privacy. But if someone reviewing our case law harbored doubts about that proposition, today's decision will do little to dissuade them."[29]

Personal Jurisdiction

In recent years, the Supreme Court has imposed significant new limits on personal jurisdiction.[30] The Court has said that "general jurisdiction" exists over a defendant in the state where the defendant is "home"; for a corporation, that is where it is incorporated or has its principal place of business. For specific jurisdiction, it must be that the defendant's contacts with the forum state gave rise to the cause of action.

In *Fuld v. Palestinian Liberation Organization*, the Court considered a statute that declared that the Palestine Liberation Organization (PLO) and the Palestinian Authority (PA) "have consented to personal jurisdiction" if they engaged in certain activities in the United States or accepted particular forms of U.S. foreign assistance.[31] The law says that they consented to personal jurisdiction "if, after a specified time, respondents 'mak[e] any payment, directly or indirectly': to anyone who has been imprisoned for committing an act of terrorism that killed a national of the United States, if such payment is made by reason of such imprisonment; or to any family member of any individual who died while committing an act of terrorism."[32]

The act also provides that the Palestine Liberation Organization and the Palestinian Authority authorized personal jurisdiction if, after a specified period, either "continues to maintain," "establishes[,] or procures any office, headquarters, premises, or other facilities or establishments in the United States," or otherwise "conducts any activity while physically present in the United States."[33]

The issue before the Supreme Court was whether this provision violated due process, an inherent limit to personal jurisdiction. In an opinion authored by the Chief Justice, the Court unanimously upheld the federal law and personal jurisdiction. The Court emphasized that this was a case in federal court, whereas most of the personal jurisdiction decisions have involved cases arising in state courts. Although the same basic principles apply, the Court explained that the concern about states' authority is not applicable when a case arises in federal court. Chief Justice Roberts stated: "Because the State and Federal Governments occupy categorically different sovereign spheres, we decline to import the Fourteenth Amendment minimum contacts standard into the Fifth Amendment. Rather, the Due Process Clause of the Fifth Amendment necessarily permits a more flexible jurisdictional inquiry commensurate with the Federal Government's broader sovereign authority."[34] But in leaving the door open, the Court said "the prospect remains that the Fifth Amendment might entail a 'similar inquiry into the reasonableness of the assertion of jurisdiction in the particular case.'"[35]

Applying this more flexible approach, the Court found that the federal statute creating personal jurisdiction did not violate due process. Chief Justice Roberts concluded that the act "reasonably ties the assertion of federal jurisdiction over the PLO and PA to conduct that involves the United States and implicates sensitive foreign policy matters within the prerogative of the political branches. We hold that the statute's provision for personal jurisdiction comports with the Due Process Clause of the Fifth Amendment."[36]

What is most fascinating about the case is the Court's explicit holding that personal jurisdiction applies differently, and with more flexibility, in federal court compared to state court. It is unclear how it will be different or what the greater flexibility will mean. But this is different from the traditional assumption that the constitutional requirements imposed by due process are the same in federal court as they are in the state courts where they are located.

Removal Jurisdiction

If a case is removed from state court to federal court and the plaintiff amends the complaint to dismiss all the federal claims, does that defeat federal court jurisdiction? That was the disputed issue in *Royal Canin USA v. Wullschleger*.[37]

Anastasia Wullschleger filed a class action suit against Royal Canin and Nestle Purina in state court for selling prescription dog food that contained no medications. Her suit alleged that the prescription requirement was misleading because the Food and Drug Administration never actually evaluated the product. The lawsuit sought damages for the higher sales price that resulted from requiring a prescription to purchase the dog food.

Royal Canin and Nestle Purina removed the case to federal court. When the case was in federal district court, Wullschleger amended her complaint and "eliminated every reference to federal law in the complaint, cut the anti-trust and unjust-enrichment claims, and narrowed her request for injunctive relief. As a replacement, she added a civil-conspiracy claim."[38] The district court nonetheless found that federal question jurisdiction still existed.

The U.S. Court of Appeals for the Eighth Circuit reversed and held that the amended complaint did not provide a basis for federal jurisdiction: "There is nothing federal about it."[39] The Eighth Circuit also said that there was not a basis for supplemental jurisdiction because there were no longer any federal claims. The court explained: "The original complaint is 'without legal effect,' meaning that the possibility of supplemental jurisdiction vanished right alongside the once-present federal questions."[40] The Court of Appeals remanded the case to state court.

The Supreme Court unanimously affirmed the Eighth Circuit. Justice Kagan wrote for the Court and explained: "When an amendment excises the federal-law claims that enabled removal, the federal court loses its supplemental jurisdiction over the related state-law claims. The case must therefore return to state court."[41] Simply put, when a case has been removed from state to federal court and the plaintiff amends the complaint to entirely eliminate the federal claims, the federal court lacks jurisdiction and must dismiss the lawsuit.

Endnotes

1. 145 S. Ct. 2540 (2025).
2. I group these cases together as they all involve issues of civil procedure and federal court jurisdiction.
3. Exec. Order No. 14160, 90 C.F.R. 8449 (2025).
4. 60 U.S. 393, 427 (1857).
5. 169 U.S. 649, 691 (1898).
6. *Id.* at 664.
7. Exec. Order No. 14160, 90 C.F.R. 8449 (2025).
8. Application for a Partial Stay of the Injunction Issued by the United States District Court for the District of Maryland at 1, 4, Trump v. CASA, Inc., 145 S. Cr. 2540 (2025) (No. 24A).
9. 145 S. Ct. 2540 (2025).
10. *Id.*
11. *Id.* at 2551.
12. *Id.* at 2553.

13. *Id.* at 2560.
14. *Id.* at 2554 n.10.
15. *Id.* at 2565 (Thomas, J., concurring).
16. *Id.* at 2366 (Alito, J., concurring).
17. *Id.* at 2570 (Kavanaugh, J., dissenting).
18. *Id.* at 2573 (Sotomayor, J., dissenting).
19. *Id.* at 2596–97 (Jackson, J., dissenting).
20. *Id.* at 2594 (Sotomayor, J., dissenting).
21. *Id.* at 2607–08 (Jackson, J., dissenting).
22. *Id.* at 2601.
23. *See* ERWIN CHEMERINSKY, FEDERAL JURISDICTION 49–50 (9th ed. 2025).
24. 145 S. Ct. 2121, 2142 (2025).
25. *Id.* at 2129.
26. *Id.* at 2130.
27. *Id.* at 2136–37.
28. *Id.* at 2149 (Jackson, J., dissenting).
29. *Id.* at 2152.
30. 145 S. Ct. 2090, 2099 (2025); *see, e.g.*, Bristol-Myers Squibb Co. v. Super. Ct. of Cal., San Francisco Cnty., 582 U.S. 255 (2017); Walden v. Fiore, 571 U.S. 277, 289–90 (2014); Daimler AG v. Bauman, 571 U.S. 117, 122 (2014).
31. 145 S. Ct. at 2100 (2025).
32. 28 U.S.C. § 2334(e)(1)(A).
33. *Id.* § 2334(e)(3).
34. 145 S. Ct. at 2105.
35. *Id.* at 2109 (quoting Asahi Metal Indus. Co. v. Super. Ct., 480 U.S. 102, 115 (1987)).
36. *Id.* at 2110.
37. 604 U.S. 22 (2025).
38. Wullschleger v. Royal Canin U.S.A., Inc., 75 F.4th 918, 921 (8th Cir. 2023).
39. *Id.* at 922.
40. *Id.* at 924 (quoting Atlas Van Lines, 209 F.3d 1064, 1067 (8th Cir. 2000)).
41. Royal Canin, 604 U.S. at 25.

Chapter 5

Civil Rights

This term the Court decided several important issues that can be grouped under "civil rights." These included cases about the standard for police liability for excessive force, the ability to sue under 42 U.S.C. § 1983, the availability of attorneys' fees under 42 U.S.C. § 1988, and an issue concerning employment discrimination under Title VII of the Civil Rights Act of 1964.

In addition to these topics, which are covered in this chapter, the Court decided an important equal protection issue in *United States v. Skrmetti*, which concerned the constitutionality of a state law prohibiting gender-affirming care for transgender youth.[1] *Skrmetti* is discussed in Chapter 8.

Also, the Court had briefing and arguments in a major case, *Louisiana v. Callais*, concerning section 2 of the Voting Rights Act, which prohibits state governments from having election systems or practices that discriminate against voters of color and against certain language minorities. However, on June 27, the Court announced that it was not deciding the case, but instead putting it over for reargument in the next term. It is discussed in Chapter 14, which looks ahead to the coming Supreme Court term.

Excessive Police Force

The Supreme Court has held that excessive police force is a seizure of a person and thus a violation of the Fourth Amendment.[2] The Supreme

Court has said that whether it is excessive force is determined from the perspective of a reasonable officer at the time of the event. In *Graham v. Connor*, in 1989, the Court said that excessive force "claims are properly analyzed under the Fourth Amendment's 'objective reasonableness' standard."[3] This means that a court will evaluate whether the force used was reasonable under the specific circumstances known to the officer at the time, not considering the officer's subjective intent or what was later learned. The focus is on what a reasonable officer, in the same situation, would have done.

In *Barnes v. Felix*, the Court considered whether the focus should be just on the moment where the force was used or whether the decision-maker should consider the surrounding context and circumstances.[4] The Court concluded that to assess whether an officer acted "reasonably in using force, a court must consider all the relevant circumstances, including facts and events leading up to the climactic moment."[5]

On April 28, 2016, Roberto Felix Jr., a law enforcement officer who was patrolling a highway outside Houston, received a "radio alert about an automobile on the road with outstanding toll violations."[6] He then spotted the car (a Toyota Corolla) and turned on his emergency lights to initiate a traffic stop. The driver, Ashtian Barnes, pulled over to the highway's shoulder.

Felix parked his car behind the Toyota Corolla, walked to the driver's side door and requested proof of insurance and a license. Barnes replied he did not have this information, that the car was a rental in his girlfriend's name, and rummaged through papers inside the car. Felix instructed Barnes to stop "digging around," commented that he "smelled marijuana," and asked if "there was anything in the car he should know about." Barnes replied that he "might have some identification in the trunk," to which Felix instructed him to open it from the seat.[7]

With his right hand resting on his holster, Felix told Barnes to get out of the car. Barnes opened the door but did not exit; instead, he turned the ignition back on. Felix unholstered his gun and, as the car began to move forward, jumped onto the car's doorsill. Felix twice shouted, "Don't fucking move" and then fired two shots into the car. Barnes was hit but managed to stop the car. Felix then radioed for backup. By the time it arrived, Barnes was dead. Five seconds had elapsed between when the car started moving and when it stopped. Within that period, two seconds passed between the moment Felix stepped on the doorsill and the moment he fired his first shot.

Barnes's mother, Janice Barnes, sued Felix on her son's behalf, alleging that Felix had violated Ashtian Barnes' Fourth Amendment rights by using excessive force against him. The lower court ruled against Barnes and in favor of the officer, applying the Fifth Circuit's approach that the focus should be only on the "moment of threat" to the police officer and not on the surrounding circumstances.

The Supreme Court unanimously reversed, holding that the moment of threat rule "constricts the proper inquiry into the 'totality of the circumstances.'"[8] Justice Elena Kagan, writing for the Court, explained that "inquiry into the reasonableness of police force requires analyzing the totality of the circumstances."[9] She stressed: "Most notable here, the totality of the circumstances inquiry into a use of force has no time limit. Of course, the situation at the precise time of the shooting will often be what matters most; it is, after all, the officer's choice in that moment that is under review. But earlier facts and circumstances may bear on how a reasonable officer would have understood and responded to later ones."[10]

It is notable that the Court does not address a "separate question about whether or how an officer's own 'creation of a dangerous situation' factors into the reasonableness analysis."[11] That issue is sure to return to the Supreme Court as it is an issue that frequently arises in police excessive force litigation.

Justice Kavanaugh wrote a concurring opinion, joined by Justices Thomas, Alito, and Barrett. Although agreeing with the result, he wrote separately to stress the dangers police officers encounter when making traffic stops. Justice Kavanaugh cited statistics regarding traffic stops turning deadly for officers.

He outlined the only options available to officers in a traffic stop when someone flees: An officer can "simply let the driver go," an officer can "give chase," an officer can attempt to "shoot out the tires," or the officer can "attempt to stop the fleeing driver at the outset by jumping on or reaching into the car" (as is the case here).[12] All are problematic and risk harm. Justice Kavanaugh concluded from this discussion that when analyzing an officer's conduct at a traffic stop when the driver suddenly pulls away, the court "must appreciate the extraordinary dangers and risks facing police officers and the community at large."[13]

Scholars have documented that it is very difficult for victims of excessive police force to recover in civil suits against the officers.[14] If the Supreme Court had taken the moment of threat approach, it would have made it even harder for victims of police misconduct to prevail. Instead, the Court reaffirmed that what is excessive force is determined from the perspective of the reasonable officer *based on the totality of the circumstances*, which includes all that gave rise to the officer's actions.

Section 1983

The Court decided two important questions concerning relief for constitutional and statutory violations under 42 U.S.C. § 1983: the ability to use it to enforce the requirements under federal spending laws and whether a state court can require exhaustion of state administrative remedies before a section 1983 suit can be filed in a state court.

Medina v. Planned Parenthood of South Carolina involved the former issue: the ability to use a section 1983 suit to enforce the requirements imposed by a law adopted under Congress's spending power.[15] There are many federal laws that appropriate money and impose conditions on recipients but do not contain an enforcement mechanism other than the cutting of federal government funds. In other words, the laws do not authorize litigation to enforce the requirements imposed by federal law.

In *Maine v. Thiboutot*, in 1980, the Court held that plaintiffs may sue under 42 U.S.C. § 1983 to enforce federal laws adopted under the spending clause.[16] The plaintiffs filed suit in state court against the State of Maine and its officers, alleging that they had violated federal statutory provisions concerning the calculation of welfare benefits. The state argued that there was no cause of action under section 1983 because that statute was available only to remedy violations of statutes protecting civil rights. The Supreme Court, in *Thiboutot*, rejected these arguments. The Court concluded that under the literal language of the statute, section 1983 suits are available whenever any federal law has been allegedly violated. The Court stated: "The question before us is whether the phrase 'and laws,' as used in § 1983, means what it says or whether it should be limited to some subset of laws. Given that Congress attached no modifiers to the phrase, the plain language of the statute undoubtedly embraces respondents' claim that petitioners violated the Social Security Act."[17]

In subsequent cases, the Supreme Court made such suits more difficult.[18] First, section 1983 may not be used to enforce statutes that explicitly or implicitly preclude section 1983 litigation. Second, the Court held that section 1983 is available only to enforce federal statutes that create rights.

Two years ago, in *Health and Hospital Corporation of Marion County v. Talevski*, the Court was asked to overrule *Maine v. Thiboutot* and end litigation under section 1983 to enforce spending clause legislation. The case involved a lawsuit brought on behalf of a patient in a county-owned nursing home claiming that its treatment of the patient violated rights guaranteed him under the Federal Nursing Home Reform Act (FNHRA).[19] The act requires that nursing homes that receive Medicaid funding respect and protect their residents' health, safety, and dignity. The law refers to rights of nursing home residents to be free from unnecessary physical or chemical restraints and to be discharged or transferred only when certain preconditions are satisfied.

The Supreme Court, in an opinion by Justice Ketanji Brown Jackson, expressly reaffirmed *Maine v. Thiboutot* and held that laws adopted under the spending clause can be enforced through section 1983 suits. Moreover, the Court said that the Federal Nursing Home Reform Act creates enforceable rights and thus can be the basis for suits under section 1983. Justice Jackson concluded the majority opinion by declaring: "Section 1983 is available to enforce every right that Congress validly and unambiguously creates; we will not impose a categorical font-of-power condition that the Reconstruction Congress did not. And, here, the test that our precedents establish leads inexorably to the conclusion that the FNHRA secures the particular rights that Talevski invokes."[20]

Medina v. Planned Parenthood of South Carolina involves the same underlying question—when can section 1983 be used to enforce the obligations of a federal spending law—but the Court came to a different result and adopted a much more restrictive approach. No state is required to participate in the Medicaid program, but states that choose to take federal Medicaid funds must meet the requirements set out in federal law.

One of these requirements is that patients can choose any qualified provider to receive medical care. Federal law requires states to ensure that "any individual eligible for medical assistance . . . may obtain" it "from any [provider] qualified to perform the service . . . who undertakes to provide" it.[21] This is meant to allow Medicaid recipients to choose their own doctors and healthcare providers.

South Carolina adopted a law preventing Planned Parenthood from receiving state Medicaid money. This was not a case about Medicaid funds being used for abortion; state and federal law already prohibited that. Rather, it was about whether women could receive other medical care from Planned Parenthood offices. The plaintiffs argued that federal law required that South Carolina allow them to use Medicaid funds for any qualified provider, including Planned Parenthood.

The Supreme Court held that the plaintiffs could not sue under section 1983 because the Medicaid statute did not clearly and unambiguously confer individual rights enforceable under section 1983. Justice Gorsuch concluded his majority opinion: "Section 1983 permits private plaintiffs to sue for violations of federal spending-power statutes only in 'atypical' situations, where the provision in question 'clear[ly]' and 'unambiguous[ly]' confers an individual 'right[.]' Section 1396a(a)(23)(A) is not such a statute."[22] The majority concluded that the only way to enforce the requirements of federal law would be for the Department of Health and Human Services to cut off federal funds to states that were not in compliance.

Justice Thomas wrote a concurring opinion urging the Court to reconsider its section 1983 jurisprudence, including as to whether the statute can be used to enforce spending clause legislation.[23] He concluded: "Given the remarkable gap between the original understanding of § 1983 and its current role, a more fundamental reexamination of our § 1983 jurisprudence is in order."[24]

Justice Jackson wrote a vehement dissent, joined by Justices Sotomayor and Kagan.[25] She spoke of the "grand ambition" of the Civil Rights Act of 1871, which enacted section 1983. She said that here it was clear that the Medicaid statute met the requirements to be deemed a law creating rights. She wrote: "Medicaid's free-choice-of-provider provision easily satisfies the unambiguous-conferral test. To start, the text of the provision is plainly 'phrased in terms of the persons benefited'—namely, Medicaid recipients. . . . Congress also used rights-creating language in the heading of the provision when it enacted the original session law. . . . And Congress reinforced its rights-creating intent by making the provision mandatory—it specifically inserted the word 'must' into the statute—to make clear that the obligation imposed on the States was binding."[26]

Justice Jackson objected to the refusal to allow suits to enforce the "free-choice-of-provider" in the Medicaid law. She said that the Court's majority opinion effectively nullified this statutory requirement; it is highly unlikely that the Department of Health and Human Services will cut off funds from states. She expressed great concern that it means that patients will not be able to get the doctors of their choice. Justice Jackson concluded her dissent:

> *The Court's decision today is not the first to so weaken the landmark civil rights protections that Congress enacted during the Reconstruction Era. That means we do have a sense of what comes next: as with those past rulings, today's decision is likely to result in tangible harm to real people. At a minimum, it will deprive Medicaid recipients in South Carolina of their only meaningful way of enforcing a right that Congress has expressly granted to them. And, more concretely, it will strip those South Carolinians—and countless other Medicaid recipients around the country—of a deeply personal freedom: the "ability to decide who treats us at our most vulnerable."*[27]

After the Court's decision in *Medina*, the issue remains as to which federal statutes can be enforced via a section 1983 suit. The Court did not completely close the door to plaintiffs using section 1983 to enforce spending clause legislation. But Justice Gorsuch said that the spending clause laws that can be enforced via section 1983 suits are "atypical exceptions."[28] Just two years before, the Court allowed such a suit in *Talevski*. It is difficult to reconcile that decision with the Court's holding in *Medina*. To be enforceable under section 1983, it must be a law that creates a right. But in both *Talevski* and *Medina* the language of the federal statutes appears to do so. The result of this confusion is likely to be a great deal more litigation as to which federal laws can be enforced through section 1983. *Medina* indicates that the Court is taking a restrictive approach.

The other case concerning section 1983, *Williams v. Reed*,[29] involved a very different issue: May a state court require exhaustion of state administration remedies before a section 1983 suit is filed in state court?

In the landmark decision, *Monroe v. Pape* in 1961, the Court held that a plaintiff may properly bring a section 1983 suit to federal court even if the state provides judicial remedies that appear completely adequate to redress the injuries.[30] In other words, a plaintiff need not exhaust state remedies before initiating a section 1983 suit in federal court. The Court explicitly declared: "The federal remedy is supplementary to the state remedy, and the latter need not be first sought and refused before the federal one is invoked."[31]

In 1982, in *Patsy v. Board of Regents*, the Court reconsidered the exhaustion issue.[32] Once again, the Court concluded that "exhaustion of state administrative remedies should not be required as a prerequisite to bringing an action pursuant to section 1983."[33] The Court explained that section 1983 created "dual or concurrent forums in the state and federal system, enabling the plaintiff to choose the forum in which to seek relief."[34] More recently, in *Knick v. Township of Scott, Pennsylvania*, in 2019, the Court reaffirmed this and held that there is no need to exhaust state administrative or judicial remedies before bringing a takings claim under section 1983.[35]

But in *Williams v. Reed*, the Alabama Supreme Court ruled that there was a need to exhaust state administrative remedies before bringing a section 1983 suit. The case involved unemployed workers in Alabama who brought suit in Alabama state court under section 1983 against the Alabama Secretary of Labor, claiming that the delay in processing their unemployment claims violated due process and violated federal statutes. The plaintiffs sought a court order requiring the Alabama Department of Labor to process their claims more quickly.

The Alabama Supreme Court ruled against the plaintiffs for failing to meet the state's requirement for exhaustion of administrative remedies. The court said that section 1983 did not preempt the state's administrative exhaustion requirement.

The Supreme Court, in a 5–4 decision, reversed the Alabama Supreme Court. Justice Brett Kavanaugh wrote for the Court, joined by Chief Justice Roberts and Justices Sotomayor, Kagan, and Jackson. Justice Kavanaugh wrote: "But that ruling created a catch-22: Because the claimants cannot sue until they complete the administrative process, they can *never* sue under § 1983 to obtain an order expediting the administrative process. This Court's precedents do not permit States to immunize state officials from § 1983 suits in that way. On that narrow ground, we reverse."[36]

It is interesting that the Court ruled narrowly on the ground that the Alabama court's exhaustion rule would preclude a section 1983 suit from ever being brought, rather than the broader—and firmly established—ground that there is no exhaustion requirement for bringing a section 1983 suit. It is also notable that Justice Thomas dissented—joined by Justices Alito, Gorsuch, and Barrett—in a case that seems so clear under well-settled law. Justice Thomas was explicit in disagreeing with Supreme Court precedents that require state courts to hear section 1983 actions. He would allow state courts to refuse to hear such claims and if they choose to do so, to impose exhaustion requirements on litigants.

In one sense, this case is significant because of what it did not do; it did not depart from long-established precedents holding that there is no exhaustion requirement before bringing a section 1983 action. Still, it is surprising that the Court emphasized it was ruling narrowly and that four justices dissented in a case that should have been clear under precedents going back to *Monroe v. Pape* over 60 years ago.

Attorneys' Fees

The law in the United States is that generally each side—winning and losing—pays its own attorneys' fees. Congress, in 1976, adopted the Civil Rights Attorney's Fees Awards Act, which provides that under federal civil rights laws, "the court, in its discretion, may allow the prevailing party, other than the United States, a reasonable attorney's fee as part of the costs."[37] The law, codified in 42 U.S.C. § 1988, was adopted to encourage lawyers to represent civil rights plaintiffs.

Lackey v. Stinnie involved the question of "whether the term 'prevailing party' in § 1988(b) encompasses a party who is awarded a preliminary injunction, if the case becomes moot before the court reaches a final judgment."[38] The case involved a suit in Virginia challenging a law that allowed for revoking drivers' licenses without due process. The plaintiffs sued and received a preliminary injunction against enforcing the Virginia law. While the case was pending, the Virginia legislature repealed the challenged law making the lawsuit moot. The plaintiffs sought attorneys' fees and the issue was whether they could receive them having won a preliminary injunction, but with the case having become moot.

Chief Justice Roberts, writing for the Court, held that attorneys' fees were not available to the plaintiffs. He wrote:

> *Because preliminary injunctions do not conclusively resolve the rights of parties on the merits, they do not confer prevailing party status. A plaintiff who secures a preliminary injunction has achieved only temporary success at an intermediary stage[ ] of the suit. It cannot yet be said that he will "ultimately prevail[ ] when the matter is finally set at rest" or that he will have "successfully maintained" his claim "at the end." And external events that render a dispute moot do not convert a temporary order designed to preserve the status of the parties into a conclusive adjudication of their rights.*[39]

Justice Jackson wrote a dissenting opinion, joined by Justice Sotomayor. She disagreed with the majority's reading of the statutory language, and she argued that it undermined Congress's goal of providing attorneys' fees to plaintiffs who substantially prevail. Plaintiffs who receive a preliminary injunction and whose suit becomes moot because the legislature changes the law in their favor should be deemed prevailing parties. Justice Jackson wrote: "Stated simply, the majority's categorical preclusion of fee awards for any plaintiff who successfully obtains preliminary injunctive relief is unwarranted. It lacks any basis in the text of § 1988(b) and is plainly inconsistent with that statutory provision's clear objective, which is to encourage attorneys to file civil rights actions on behalf of the most vulnerable people in our society. The Court has now eliminated fee eligibility for *all* preliminary injunctions—even those that effectively resolve the case."[40] She concluded: "There is no persuasive reason to believe that Congress meant to preclude fee awards for every plaintiff who secures preliminary injunctive relief but not a final judgment, no matter the context."[41]

There is no doubt that this decision will be harmful to civil rights plaintiffs in precluding them from recovering attorneys' fees in situations like this where they prevail with a preliminary injunction, but then the case becomes moot. Chief Justice Roberts expressly praised the result for creating a bright-line rule.[42] But it is a bright-line rule that will very much favor defendants and limit the ability of plaintiffs to recover attorneys' fees in these situations.

Title VII

Title VII of the 1964 Civil Rights Act prohibits employment discrimination based on race, sex, or religion. In *Bostock v. Clayton County, Georgia*, the Supreme Court held that the prohibition of sex discrimination included forbidding discrimination based on sex or gender identity.[43]

In *Ames v. Department of Youth Services*, the Supreme Court held that the burdens of proof under Title VII are the same regardless of the sexual orientation of the plaintiff.[44] More generally, the Court said that the burdens are the same on all plaintiffs, whether they are in a "majority" or a "minority" group.

In 2004, the Ohio Department of Youth Services agency hired petitioner Marlean Ames, a heterosexual woman, to serve as an executive secretary. Ames was eventually promoted to program administrator and, in 2019, applied for a newly created management position in the agency's Office of Quality and Improvement. Although the agency interviewed her for the position, it ultimately hired a different candidate—a lesbian woman—to fill the role.

A few days after Ames interviewed for the management position, her supervisors removed her from her role as program administrator. She was demoted to the secretarial role she had held when she first joined the agency—a move that resulted in a significant pay cut. The agency then hired a gay man to fill the vacant program administrator position.

Ames subsequently filed this lawsuit against the agency under Title VII, alleging that she was denied the management promotion and demoted because of her sexual orientation. The federal district court ruled against Ames and the U.S. Court of Appeals for the Sixth Circuit affirmed. The

Sixth Circuit held that Ames had failed to meet her prima facie burden because she had not shown "background circumstances to support the suspicion that the defendant is that unusual employer who discriminates against the majority."[45] The court reasoned that Ames, as a straight woman, was required to make this showing "in addition to the usual ones for establishing a prima-facie case."[46]

The issue was whether those in a majority group have to meet an additional burden in Title VII litigation. The Supreme Court unanimously reversed the lower courts and held that the burdens are the same under Title VII regardless of whether one is part of a majority or a minority group. Justice Jackson wrote the opinion for the Court and explained that the Sixth Circuit's "background circumstances" rule—which requires members of a majority group to satisfy a heightened evidentiary standard to prevail on a Title VII claim—cannot be squared with the text of Title VII or the Court's precedent. She explained that Title VII's disparate-treatment provision bars employers from intentionally discriminating against their employees on the "basis of race, color, religion, sex, or national origin" and "draws no distinctions between majority-group plaintiffs and minority-group plaintiffs."[47]

The holding in the case is not surprising, nor is the unanimity. But the decision is important in resolving a split among the lower courts. Although the decision is about sexual orientation discrimination, the holding surely applies to all types of claims under Title VII.

Endnotes

1. 145 S. Ct. 1816 (2025).
2. *See* Graham v. Connor, 490 U.S. 386 (1989); Tennessee v. Garner, 471 U.S. 1 (1985).
3. Graham v. Connor, 490 U.S. at 388.
4. 145 S. Ct. 1353 (2025).
5. *Id.* at 1356.
6. *Id.*
7. *Id.*
8. *Id.*
9. *Id.* at 1358.
10. *Id.*

11. *Id.* at 1361.
12. *Id.* at 1362 (Kavanaugh, J., concurring).
13. *Id.* at 1363.
14. Osagie Obasogie & Zachary Newman, *The Futile Fourth Amendment: Understanding Excessive Police Force Doctrine Through an Empirical Assessment of Graham v. Connor*, 112 Nw. U. L. Rev. 1465 (2018).
15. 145 S. Ct. 2219 (2025).
16. 448 U.S. 1 (1980).
17. *Id.* at 4.
18. The law concerning these exceptions is reviewed in Erwin Chemerinsky, Federal Jurisdiction, ch. 8 (8th ed. 2020).
19. 143 S. Ct. 1444 (2023).
20. *Id.* at 1462.
21. 42 U.S.C. § 1396(c).
22. *Medina*, 145 S. Ct. at 2239.
23. *Id.* at 2239–40 (Thomas, J., dissenting).
24. *Id.* at 2246.
25. *Id.* (Jackson, J., dissenting).
26. *Id.* at 2252.
27. *Id.* at 2258.
28. *Id.* at 2239.
29. 145 S. Ct. 465 (2025).
30. 365 U.S. 167 (1961).
31. *Id.* at 183.
32. 457 U.S. 496 (1982).
33. *Id.* at 516.
34. *Id.* at 506.
35. 139 S. Ct. 2162 (2019); *see also* Pakdel v. City & Cnty. of S.F., 594 U.S. 474, 475 (2021) ("Exhaustion of state remedies is not a prerequisite to an action under 42 U.S.C. § 1983.").
36. Williams v. Reed, 145 S. Ct. at 467.
37. 42 U.S.C. § 1988.
38. 145 S. Ct. 659, 666 (2025).
39. *Id.* at 667–68.
40. *Id.* at 671–72 (Jackson, J., dissenting).
41. *Id.* at 672.
42. 145 S. Ct. at 669.
43. 140 S. Ct. 1731 (2020).
44. 145 S. Ct. 1540 (2025).
45. 87 F.4th 822, 825 (CA6 2023).
46. *Id.*
47. 145 S. Ct. at 1546.

Chapter 6

Criminal Law and Procedure

As explained in Chapter 1, the overall size of the Supreme Court's docket has decreased greatly over time, falling from over 160 cases a term in the 1980s to this year's 56 decisions. Interestingly, the number of significant criminal law and criminal procedure cases has fallen even more.[1] Again this term, like the last several, there have been no decisions about searches and seizures,[2] and no cases about the privilege against self-incrimination, the confrontation clause, or eyewitness identifications.

There is no clear explanation for the dearth of important criminal law and criminal procedure cases. Perhaps, in part, as explained in Chapter 1, it is how few cases review state court decisions. In October Term 2024, only three of 56 decisions involved Supreme Court review of state court rulings. Likely, too, this reflects the absence of new federal criminal laws in recent years. When Congress adopts criminal statutes, often there is a need for interpretation. And perhaps it is simply that the justices, at this point, are less interested in criminal law and procedure than other matters.

Three cases concerning criminal law and procedure seem especially important from this term. *Glossip v. Oklahoma* concerned the right to a new trial in a death penalty case where the prosecutor used false testimony.[3] *Andrew v. White* involved when due process is violated by the use of prejudicial testimony.[4] *Thompson v. United States* focused on whether the federal statute that prohibits false statements applies to statements that are misleading but true.[5]

Glossip v. Oklahoma

Richard Glossip was convicted of murder in Oklahoma and sentenced to death. Justin Sneed, who beat the victim to death, testified at trial that Glossip offered Sneed thousands of dollars to commit the murder to get the victim's money. Sneed's testimony was all that linked Glossip to the murder. Glossip confessed he helped Sneed conceal his crime after the fact, but he denied any involvement in the murder. At the trial, Sneed denied that he was taking lithium to treat a bipolar condition. The State, in subsequent investigations, learned this to be false testimony.

Glossip continually maintained his innocence and filed many petitions for post-conviction relief in both federal and state court. These drew the attention of the Oklahoma legislature, which hired the firm of Reed Smith to do an investigation.[6] In June 2022, Reed Smith reported its "grave doubt as to the integrity of Glossip's murder conviction and death sentence."[7] Among other things, Reed Smith concluded the prosecution had "deliberately destroyed 'key physical evidence' before Glossip's retrial, including several items from the crime scene and the inn's receipts and deposit books, which could have helped Glossip address the accusations of embezzlement."[8] Reed Smith also concluded that crucial testimony about Glossip's actions had been provided by a former police officer of "very limited honesty and integrity" who was jailed for making false statements shortly after Glossip's second trial.[9]

Two months after Reed Smith provided its report, the prosecutors disclosed seven boxes of evidence that had been withheld at Glossip's trial.[10] Glossip filed a petition for post-conviction relief in the Oklahoma Court of Criminal Appeals based on the Reed Smith report and the newly discovered material. Soon after, the State found an eighth box of evidence. This revealed that the prosecutor had elicited false testimony at trial from Sneed, where he denied taking lithium for bipolar disorder. Glossip filed a petition for post-conviction relief with the Oklahoma Supreme Court based on this new information.

The Attorney General of Oklahoma supported Glossip's petition, conceding multiple errors that warranted a new trial. But the Oklahoma Court of Criminal Appeals denied the unopposed petition without a hearing, holding that Glossip's claims were procedurally barred under Oklahoma's Post-Conviction Procedures Act because this was an impermissible successive petition for relief. The court also said that the State's concession was not "based in law or fact" and did not show a constitutional violation.[11]

The Supreme Court reversed the Oklahoma Court of Criminal Appeals and ordered that there be a new trial. Justice Sonia Sotomayor wrote for the majority. Justice Clarence Thomas wrote a dissenting opinion, which was joined by Justice Alito and, in part, by Justice Barrett. Justice Gorsuch did not participate in the case.

A threshold question for the Court was whether it could review the Oklahoma Court of Criminal Appeal's decision. The Supreme Court cannot review a state court decision that rests on an independent and adequate state law ground of decision.[12] The argument was that the Oklahoma Court of Criminal Appeals relied on Oklahoma law preventing successive petitions for post-conviction relief. But the U.S. Supreme Court rejected this argument. Under *Michigan v. Long*, if a statute is ambiguous, the Supreme Court will assume that there is not an independent and adequate state ground of decision; a state court must make clear that it is relying on such a ground of decision.[13] The Supreme Court said that it was not "clear from the face of the opinion" below that the state court was relying on an independent state law ground and thus, we must "accept as the most reasonable explanation that the state court decided the case the way it did because it believed that federal law required it to do so."[14]

On the merits, the Supreme Court applied *Napue v. Illinois*, which held that a conviction knowingly "obtained through use of false evidence" violates the 14th Amendment's due process clause.[15] Justice Sotomayor explained:

> *To establish a Napue violation, a defendant must show that the prosecution knowingly solicited false testimony or knowingly allowed it "to go uncorrected when it appear[ed]." If the defendant makes that showing, a new trial is warranted so long as the false testimony "may have had an effect on the outcome of the trial,"—that is, if it "in any reasonable*

> *likelihood [could] have affected the judgment of the jury." In effect, this materiality standard requires "the beneficiary of [the] constitutional error to prove beyond a reasonable doubt that the error complained of did not contribute to the verdict obtained."*[16]

The Supreme Court, noting that the Oklahoma Attorney General agreed, found that there was a *Napue* violation: The prosecution knowingly used false testimony that was material to the verdict. The Court stated, "[f]or these reasons, we conclude that the prosecution's failure to correct Sneed's trial testimony violated the Due Process Clause. Glossip is entitled to a new trial."[17]

Justice Amy Coney Barrett, concurred in part and dissented in part.[18] She agreed that the Supreme Court could hear the matter and that there was a violation of *Napue v. Illinois*, but she would have remanded the case to the Oklahoma Supreme Court to decide if a new trial was warranted.

Justice Thomas wrote a strong dissent, joined by Justice Alito and in part by Justice Barrett.[19] Thomas said he would have denied review of the Oklahoma Court of Criminal Appeals decision and disagreed that there was a *Napue* violation. He wrote:

> *The Oklahoma Court of Criminal Appeals (OCCA) denied Glossip's application as both procedurally deficient and non-meritorious, and Oklahoma's Pardon and Parole Board denied clemency. Because this Court lacks the power to override these denials, that should have marked the end of the road for Glossip. Instead, the Court stretches the law at every turn to rule in his favor. At the threshold, it concocts federal jurisdiction by misreading the decision below. On the merits, it finds a due process violation based on patently immaterial testimony about a witness's medical condition. And, for the remedy, it orders a new trial in violation of black-letter law on this Court's power to review state-court judgments.*[20]

The Supreme Court's decision in *Glossip v. Oklahoma* does not make new law. The Court applied long-standing precedents, *Michigan v. Long* and *Napue v. Illinois*, to hold that it could hear the case and that it is reversible error for a prosecutor to knowingly use false testimony. The case is important in reaffirming these decisions. *Napue* is not a case that has received much attention and the Court's decision in *Glossip* is likely to increase its importance.

Perhaps what is most interesting about the decision in *Glossip v. Oklahoma* is its procedural context: the state joined with the defendant in urging a new trial, but the state highest court refused relief. The U.S. Supreme Court, which relatively rarely rules in favor of those facing a death sentence, did so here.

Andrew v. White

An Oklahoma jury convicted Brenda Andrew of murdering her husband, Rob Andrew, and sentenced her to death. Rob purchased a $800,000 life insurance policy, with Brenda named as the beneficiary. Brenda and James Pavatt then began an affair, and Brenda initiated divorce proceedings.

Rob later discovered his brakes were cut from his car. In response, Brenda remarked to Rob that she had read about his brakes being cut in the newspaper, however Rob found that no such article existed.[21]

Thinking that Brenda and Pavatt were going to kill him, Rob sought to remove Brenda as his life insurance beneficiary.

On November 20, 2001, Rob came to pick up his two children at Brenda's home and Brenda asked him to help her light a pilot light in the garage. As Andrew walked into the garage, two men shot and killed Rob with a 16-gauge shotgun. Brenda was superficially shot in the arm by a .22 caliber gun, and she told the police that two armed assailants had committed the shooting.

Brenda, who skipped her husband's funeral, asked Pavatt's grown daughter to forge Rob's signature on documents to allow her children to leave the country.[22] Pavatt, Brenda, and her children then traveled to Mexico together, but after three months, the couple ran out of money and returned home to the U.S. where they were arrested. Pavatt confessed to committing the shooting with a friend but denied that Brenda had been involved.

The State thereafter charged both Pavatt and Brenda with capital murder. A jury convicted Pavatt and sentenced him to death. At Brenda's trial, the prosecution sought to prove that Brenda had conspired with Pavatt, an insurance agent, to murder her husband for the proceeds of his life insurance policy.

The prosecution elicited testimony "about [Brenda]'s sexual partners reaching back two decades; about the outfits she wore to dinner or during grocery runs; about the underwear she packed for vacation; and about how often she had sex in her car."[23] In its closing statement, the prosecution again invoked these themes, displaying Andrew's "thong underwear" to the jury and reminding them of Brenda's alleged affairs during college and with Pavatt. The jury convicted Brenda and sentenced her to death.

After exhausting her state appeals, Brenda filed a petition for a writ of habeas corpus in federal court. The lower courts ruled against her, but the Supreme Court in per curiam opinion reversed and ruled in her favor. Justice Alito concurred in the judgment, while Justice Thomas wrote a dissent, which was joined by Justice Gorsuch.

The Court said that *Payne v. Tennessee* announced the legal principle that due process is violated by the "introduction of unduly prejudicial evidence at a criminal trial."[24] The Court said that although *Payne* was in a different context—it concerned when victim impact statements are permissible[25]—it is a principle well established in the law. The Court explained that "*Payne* did not invent due process protections against unduly prejudicial evidence. The Court had several times before held that prosecutors' prejudicial or misleading statements violate due process if they render a trial or capital sentencing fundamentally unfair. . . . By the time of the [Oklahoma Court of Criminal Appeal's] decision in this case, it was clear that the introduction of unduly prejudicial evidence could, in certain cases, violate the Due Process Clause."[26]

The Supreme Court said that the Tenth Circuit erred in concluding that there was not clearly established law and remanded the case for it to apply due process to the facts.

Justice Alito wrote a short opinion concurring in the judgment that a defendant's due process rights can be violated when "the properly admitted evidence at trial is overwhelmed by a flood of irrelevant and highly prejudicial evidence that renders the trial fundamentally unfair."[27]

Justice Thomas, in a dissent joined by Justice Gorsuch, disagreed with the majority's conclusion that *Payne v. Tennessee* provided a legal precedent that could be the basis for federal habeas corpus relief.[28] He stressed that *Payne* was a case about when victim impact statements at sentencing violate the Constitution. He said that *Payne*'s "lone sentence on due process" does not provide a test for the determination of when a trial is "so infected by prejudicial evidence as to be fundamentally unfair."[29]

The Court's decision in *Andrew v. White* is important in holding that *Payne v. Tennessee*, which is usually thought of as a case about victim impact statements and the Eighth Amendment, also establishes a rule under due process. The Court says that *Payne* holds that the introduction of unduly prejudicial evidence violates due process. And the Court deems that this is sufficiently established to be able to be raised on federal habeas corpus. Although this is not a case that received much media attention, it will be very important in criminal cases and habeas litigation.

Thompson v. United States

Does a federal law that prohibits false statements apply to statements that are true, but misleading? This was the issue in *Thompson v. United States.*[30]

Between 2011 and 2014, Patrick Thompson took out three loans from the Washington Federal Bank for Savings, resulting in a total loan balance of $219,000. In 2017, the Bank failed, and the FDIC became responsible for collecting the Bank's outstanding loans. As part of that process, the FDIC's loan servicer—Planet Home Lending—sent Thompson an invoice in February 2018 listing a balance due of $269,120.58, the $219,000 Thompson had borrowed plus interest.

On February 23, 2018, Thompson called the customer service line of Planet Home Lending. During a recorded call, Thompson told the customer service agent that he had "no idea where the 269 number comes from," that he "borrowed the money, I owe the money—but I borrowed . . . I think it was $110,000."[31] On March 1, 2018, in a non-recorded call with two FDIC contractors, Thompson mentioned borrowing $110,000 for "home improvement" before both parties "ultimately agreed to settle Thompson's debt for $219,000—the principal amount of his loans."[32]

Thompson was later indicted under 18 U.S.C. § 1014, which prohibits "knowingly mak[ing] any false statement" in an attempt to influence the FDIC's actions on any loan.[33] Thompson argued that his statements were not false because he had in fact taken out a loan for $110,000, as he had said. The district court and the Seventh Circuit held that they did not need to consider that argument because the prohibition in section 1014 against false statements extends to "misleading ones as well," and Thompson's statements were "at least misleading in failing to mention the additional loans."[34]

The Supreme Court unanimously reversed the lower courts and held that section 1014 does not criminalize statements that are "misleading but true."[35] The judgment of the Court of Appeals for the Seventh Circuit was vacated, and the case remanded for further proceedings consistent with the opinion.

Chief Justice Roberts wrote for the Court and reasoned that "false" and "misleading" are two different things: A misleading statement can be true.[36] The Court concluded: "In casual conversation, people use many overlapping words to describe shady statements: false, misleading, dishonest, deceptive, literally true, and more. Only one of those words appears in the statute. Section 1014 does not criminalize statements that are misleading but true. Under the statute, it is not enough that a statement is misleading. It must be 'false.'"[37]

Many federal laws prohibit false statements. *Thompson v. United States* is important in holding that a federal law prohibits just false, but not misleading, statements and applies only if there is the requisite proof of falsity. Showing that statements were misleading, even intentionally so, is not enough for conviction under such laws.

Endnotes

1. Many cases, though, involve the constitutionality of criminal statutes and are discussed elsewhere in this book. For example, *United States v. Skrmetti*, 145 S. Ct. 1816 (2025) involved the constitutionality of a Tennessee law prohibiting gender-affirming care for transgender youth (discussed in Chapter 8), and *Free Speech Coal. v. Paxton*, 145 S. Ct. 2291 (2025) involved the constitutionality of a Texas law requiring age verification for websites with significant sexually explicit content (discussed in Chapter 10). In this chapter, I am focusing on what are traditionally regarded as issues of criminal law and procedure.

2. There was one case concerning the Fourth Amendment: *Barnes v. Felix*, 145 S. Ct. 1353 (2025). It concerned the standard for determining whether there is excessive police force that violates the Fourth Amendment. It is discussed in Chapter 5, which focuses on civil rights.

3. Glossip v. Oklahoma, 145 S. Ct. 612 (2025).

4. Andrew v. White, 145 S. Ct. 75 (2025).

5. Thompson v. United States, 145 S. Ct. 821 (2025).

6. *Glossip*, 145 S. Ct. at 621.

7. *Id.*

8. *Id.*

9. *Id.*

10. *Id.*

11. *Id.* at 624.

12. *See* Erwin Chemerinsky, Federal Jurisdiction ch. 10 (9th ed. 2025).

13. Michigan v. Long, 463 U.S. 1032 (1983).

14. *Glossip*, 145 S. Ct. at 624.

15. Napue v. Illinois, 360 U.S. 264, 269 (1959).

16. *Glossip*, 145 S. Ct. at 626–27 (citations omitted).

17. *Id.* at 630.

18. *Id.* at 633 (Barrett, J., concurring in part and dissenting in part).

19. *Id.* at 636 (Thomas, J., dissenting).

20. *Id.*

21. Andrew v. White, 145 S. Ct. at 84.

22. *Id.* at 85.

23. *Id.* at 78–79.

24. *Id.* at 81.

25. *See* Payne v. Tennessee, 501 U.S. 808 (1991).

26. Andrew v. White, 145 S. Ct. at 81.

27. *Id.* at 83 (Alito, J., concurring).

28. *Id.* (Thomas, J., dissenting).

29. *Id.* at 89.

30. Thompson v. United States, 145 S. Ct. at 825–26.

31. *Id.* at 824.

32. *Id.* at 824–25.

33. 18 U.S.C. § 1014.

34. *Thompson*, 145 S. Ct. at 824; *see* United States v. Thompson, 89 F.4th 1010 (7th Cir. 2024).

35. *Thompson*, 145 S. Ct. at 828–29.

36. *Id.* at 825.

37. *Id.* at 828–29.

Chapter 7

Environmental Law

The Court decided several cases concerning environmental law. All involved statutory interpretation of federal laws regulating the environment. In each, the Court rejected the position favored by environmentalists. Two that seem particularly important involved the National Environmental Policy Act and the federal Water Pollution Control Act.[1]

National Environmental Policy Act and Environmental Impact Statements

The National Environmental Policy Act (NEPA), adopted in 1969, requires federal agencies to assess the environmental effects of their proposed major actions and to involve the public in the decision-making process. NEPA seeks to ensure that environmental issues are considered in decisions by federal agencies. The act requires that there be environmental impact statements (EISs) to help make sure that environmental considerations are taken into account.

The Seven County Infrastructure Coalition sought to construct a new 88-mile railroad line connecting Utah's oil-rich Uinta Basin to the national rail network in order to transport crude oil to refineries along the Gulf Coast. To obtain a certificate of approval from the Surface Transportation

Board, as required under NEPA, the Coalition submitted an EIS.[2] The EIS amounted to over 3,600 pages of environmental analysis.

The board subsequently approved the railroad line in December 2021, concluding that the project's "substantial transportation and economic benefits" outweighed the environmental impacts identified in the EIS.[3] A Colorado county and several environmental organizations then filed challenges to the board's approval in the U.S. Court of Appeals for the District of Columbia Circuit, claiming the EIS did not sufficiently consider the environmental effects of projects separate from the railroad line itself.

The D.C. Circuit vacated both the EIS and board's approval of the railroad, holding that neither sufficiently considered the "reasonably foreseeable" environmental effects that could ensue from (1) increased oil drilling upstream in the Uinta Basin and (2) increased oil refining downstream along the Gulf Coast of Louisiana and Texas.[4] The D.C. Circuit found that the board impermissibly limited its analysis, and the EIS should have been analyzed more extensively.

In *Seven County Infrastructure Coalition v. Eagle County, Colorado*,[5] in an 8–0 decision, with the majority opinion delivered by Justice Kavanaugh, the Supreme Court reversed and remanded, declaring that the "central principle of judicial review in NEPA cases is deference."[6] Kavanaugh was joined by Justices Roberts, Alito, and Barrett. The Court found that the D.C. Circuit incorrectly interpreted NEPA by failing to afford the substantial judicial deference it requires: "NEPA is a procedural cross-check, not a substantive roadblock."[7] As a "purely procedural" statute, NEPA requires agencies to focus on the environmental effects of the project at issue, not those separate from it. The Court reasoned that a "separate project breaks the chain of proximate causation between the project at hand and the environmental effects of the separate project."[8] Accordingly, "adequacy of an EIS is relevant only to the question of whether an agency's final decision (here, to approve the railroad project) was reasonably explained."[9]

Justice Kavanaugh wrote:

> *So long as the EIS addresses environmental effects from the project at issue, courts should defer to agencies' decisions about where to draw the line—including (i) how far to go in*

> *considering indirect environmental effects from the project at hand and (ii) whether to analyze environmental effects from other projects separate in time or place from the project at hand. On those kinds of questions, as this Court has often said, agencies possess discretion and must have broad latitude to draw a "manageable line."*[10]

Justice Kavanaugh expressed concern that NEPA has become a "tool employed by project opponents (who may not always be entirely motivated by concern for the environment) to try to stop or at least slow down new infrastructure and construction projects."[11] He describes NEPA as "a 1970 legislative acorn [that] has grown over the years into a judicial oak that has hindered infrastructure development under the guise of [judicial review]."[12]

The Court's professing the need for courts to defer to the Environmental Protection Agency (EPA) is in marked contrast to its ruling a year earlier in *Loper Bright Enterprises v. Raimondo*, where the Court overruled *Chevron* deference to agencies when they are interpreting ambiguous statutes.[13] Here, by contrast, the Court expresses the need for judicial deference to agencies when it comes to environmental impact statements. Of course, the context is different, yet there is a striking difference in the Court's view of the desirability of deferring to agency expertise.

Clean Water Act

Under the Clean Water Act (CWA), a National Pollutant Discharge Elimination System (NPDES) permit is required to lawfully discharge pollutants into covered bodies of water.[14] Under section 1311 of the CWA, the EPA may condition permits based on certain "effluent limitations."

In 2019, a wastewater treatment facility owned by the city of San Francisco was issued a NPDES renewal permit that included two new limitation requirements. The provisions prohibited discharging anything that (1) causes or contributes to a violation of "any applicable water quality standard" for receiving waters, or (2) "creates pollution, contamination, or nuisance as defined by California Water Code section 13050."

San Francisco appealed to the EPA's Environmental Appeals Board, arguing that these "end-result" requirements were not authorized by section 1311(b)(1)(C) of the CWA. End-result requirements make the permittee responsible for the quality of the water it discharges pollutants into, as opposed to spelling out what to do or refrain from doing. The city contended that this could not be reconciled with section 1342(k)'s permit shield provision, which protects permittees who are compliant to the terms of their permit from liability.[15] The Environmental Appeals Board rejected the challenge, prompting the city to then seek review in the Ninth Circuit. San Francisco's position was supported by several other similarly situated cities, including New York, the District of Columbia, Boston, and Buffalo.

The issue in *City and County of San Francisco v. EPA* involves determining whether section 1311(b)(1)(C) provides the EPA with the statutory authority to condition compliance on the quality of water through end-result requirements.

The U.S. Court of Appeals for the Ninth Circuit denied the city's petition for review, holding that section 1311(b)(1)(C) authorizes the EPA to impose "*any* more stringent limitation" to ensure water quality standards are satisfied.[16]

In a 5–4 decision, with the majority opinion delivered by Justice Alito, the Supreme Court reversed, holding that the EPA was not authorized to include end-result provisions in NPDES permits. Joined in part by Justices Roberts, Thomas, and Kavanaugh, the Court relied on a fairness argument, expressing concern that entities could be heavily penalized without notice of obligation to take any specific step. As Justice Alito put it, a permittee who "punctiliously follows every specific requirement in its permit may nevertheless face crushing penalties if the quality of the water in its receiving waters falls below the applicable standards."[17]

The Court said that the EPA's responsibility is to determine what steps permittees must take to ensure adequate water quality standards are met, not work "backward from pollution to assign responsibility."[18] Justice Alito used an interesting metaphor to explain his reading of section 1311(b)(1)(C): "A reference to 'any mammal' would capture all mammals, but it would not encompass a bird or fish. Similarly, § 1311(b)(1)(C) encompasses any *limitation* that is necessary to meet or implement water quality standards, but not provisions that do not fall within that category."[19]

The Court also looked to legislative history, determining that with the 1972 refurbishment of the CWA, "Congress deliberately deleted a long-standing provision that expressly authorized what the dissent wishes to perpetuate."[20] The intentionality behind removing this "major defect in the old scheme" was further supported by an absence of any provided mechanism to allocate responsibility for water quality violations among multiple dischargers.

Justice Barrett, dissenting in part, was joined by Justices Sotomayor, Kagan, and Jackson. The dissent found the Court's reading of "limitation" to be wrong as a matter of ordinary English.[21] End-result requirements are plainly "limitations" and thus authorized by section 1311(b)(1)(C). Justice Barrett explained their importance in controlling water pollution and fulfilling the goals of the Water Pollution Control Act.

Endnotes

1. The Court also decided *Diamond Alternative Energy LLC v. EPA*, 145 S. Ct. 2121 (2025), which involved standing of fossil fuel producers to challenge an EPA waiver under the Clean Air Act to allow California to require more electric cars. This case is discussed in Chapter 4.
2. Seven Cnty. Infrastructure Coal. v. Eagle Cnty., Colo., 145 S. Ct. 1497 (2025).
3. *Id.* at 1509.
4. Eagle Cnty. v. Colo Seven Cnty. Infrastructure Coal., 82 F.4th 1152 (2023).
5. 145 S. Ct. 1497 (2025).
6. *Id.* at 1511.
7. *Id.* at 1507.
8. *Id.* at 1516.
9. *Id.* at 1513.
10. *Id.*
11. *Id.*
12. *Id.* at 1514.
13. Loper Bright Enters. v. Raimondo, 144 S. Ct. 2244 (2024).
14. 33 U.S.C. 26 § 1342.
15. *Id.*
16. City & Cnty. of San Francisco v. EPA, 75 F.4th 1074, 1089 (2023).

17. 145 S. Ct. at 710.
18. *Id.* at 716.
19. *Id.*
20. *Id.* at 717 n.12.
21. *Id.* at 723 (Barrett, J., concurring dissenting in part).

Chapter 8

Equal Protection

The culture wars came to the Supreme Court in *United States v. Skrmetti*, which involves the constitutionality of a Tennessee law that prohibits gender-affirming care for transgender youth.[1] As of July 2025, 27 states have adopted laws like those in Tennessee.[2] Not surprisingly, given how the issue has become politicized, all of these states are controlled by Republican state legislatures.[3] The Human Rights Campaign estimates that 120,400 transgender teenagers, about 40 percent of transgender youth, live in states with bans on gender-affirming care.[4]

The legal issue centered on what level of constitutional scrutiny should be used for such state laws. Should it be rational basis review with great deference to the Tennessee legislature or should it be heightened scrutiny and much greater protection for transgender youth? Underlying the case is a cultural divide about gender identity, transgender individuals, and the practical implications of these laws on the lives of transgender youth.

The Tennessee Law

The Tennessee statute, SB1, prohibits healthcare providers from "[p]rescribing, administering, or dispensing any puberty blocker or hormone" to enable "a minor to identify with, or live as, a purported identity inconsistent with the minor's sex" or "treat purported discomfort or distress from a discordance between the minor's sex and asserted identity."[5] SB1 defines "[s]ex" as the "immutable characteristics of the reproductive system that define the individual as male or female, as determined by anatomy and genetics existing at the time of birth."[6] The law also prohibits surgical procedures provided for the same purposes, but that prohibition is not at issue in this case and surgical procedures are, nonetheless, rarely performed on minors.

Those who violate the Tennessee law may be punished through $25,000 civil penalties per each prohibited prescription or treatment, by professional discipline, and through any potential civil liability in private suits. In other states with similar legislation, there are criminal penalties for health professionals who prescribe puberty-blocking drugs or cross-sex hormones.

On the other side of the coin—exemplifying the cultural divide over this issue—16 states and the District of Columbia have shield laws that protect access to gender-affirming care for transgender youth. These laws are written to affirm a minor's right to receive gender-affirming care and to protect patients, guardians, and medical professionals from prosecution for seeking or providing related care.

The Litigation

The petitioners before the Supreme Court were the United States government and three transgender adolescents from Tennessee, their parents, and a Tennessee doctor who treats adolescents with gender dysphoria. After the inauguration, the Trump administration told the Court it was changing positions and was supporting the constitutionality of the Tennessee law, but it did not ask for the case's dismissal. The new administration likely predicted, based on the oral arguments that had already occurred, that the Court was prepared to side with its position to uphold the Tennessee law.

The federal district court found that SB1 was likely unconstitutional because it denied equal protection and therefore issued a preliminary injunction.[7] The district court concluded that the Tennessee law discriminated based on sex and gender identity. The district court thus applied intermediate scrutiny, which requires that a government action be substantially related to an important government interest. The court concluded that the Tennessee law prohibited administration of the prevailing standard of care to transgender youth. The court explained "the weight of the evidence" did not support the State's contention that "either puberty blockers or cross-sex hormones pose serious risks" to transgender adolescents.[8] At the same time, the court found that "the benefits of the medical procedures banned by SB1 are well-established."[9] Finding that the Tennessee law would cause irreparable injury, the district court issued a preliminary injunction.

The U.S. Court of Appeals for the Sixth Circuit, in a 2–1 decision, reversed the district court.[10] The Sixth Circuit said that only rational basis review was appropriate for the law. The Court of Appeals said that the law is not sex discrimination because it "regulate[s] sex-transition treatments for all minors regardless of sex."[11] The court said that discrimination against transgender individuals does not warrant heightened scrutiny.

Applying rational basis review, the Sixth Circuit concluded that the Tennessee law was reasonable in light of the medical uncertainties in administering puberty-blocking hormones to transgender youth. The court stressed the appropriateness of judicial deference to the legislature in this area.

The Supreme Court's Decision

In a 6–3 decision, split along ideological lines, the Supreme Court upheld the Tennessee law. Chief Justice John Roberts wrote the opinion for the majority, while Justices Clarence Thomas, Samuel Alito, and Amy Coney Barrett wrote concurring opinions. Justice Sonia Sotomayor wrote a scathing dissent, joined by Justices Elena Kagan and Ketanji Brown Jackson. Justice Kagan also wrote a short, separate dissent.

Chief Justice Roberts stressed the need for the court to defer to the judgment of the Tennessee legislature. He concluded his opinion by saying that the issue is left "to the people, their elected representatives, and the democratic process."[12] Likewise, Justice Clarence Thomas, in a concurring opinion, said: "Deference to legislatures, not experts, is particularly critical here."[13]

The Court's deference was based on its conclusion that rational basis review, rather than heightened scrutiny, was appropriate. The challengers to the Tennessee law argued that intermediate scrutiny was warranted for two separate reasons: sex discrimination and discrimination based on gender identity. The Court rejected both arguments, with the dissenting justices strongly disagreeing with the majority's conclusions as to each.

As for the former proposition, the Court said that the Tennessee law was not sex discrimination because it prohibited all children, regardless of their sex, from receiving puberty-blocking hormones or cross-sex hormones for the purpose of facilitating a gender transition. Chief Justice Roberts wrote: "Neither of the above classifications turns on sex. Rather, SB1 prohibits healthcare providers from administering puberty blockers and hormones to *minors* for certain *medical uses*, regardless of a minor's sex."[14]

In her dissent, Justice Sotomayor said that this ruling ignores that the law allows some drugs to be given to boys and not girls, and some to girls and not boys. A boy could be given testosterone to develop male characteristics; but a girl could not be given that drug to do so. A girl could be given estrogen to develop female characteristics; but a boy could not be given the drug for those reasons. Justice Sotomayor said that, by definition, that is sex discrimination. She explained it this way in her dissenting opinion: "Sex determines access to the covered medication. Physicians in Tennessee can prescribe hormones and puberty blockers to help a male child, but not a female child, look more like a boy; and to help a female child, but not a male child, look more like a girl."[15]

The dissent said that *Bostock v. Clayton County, Georgia* shows that discrimination based on gender identity is sex discrimination.[16] In that case, the Supreme Court held that discrimination against transgender individuals in employment is sex discrimination that violates Title VII. A transgender woman would have kept her job only if she was male. But the majority in *Skrmetti* disputed the relevance of the Title VII analysis for deciding the equal protection issue.

Second, the challengers argued that the law discriminates against transgender youth and that discrimination based on gender identity should receive intermediate scrutiny. Chief Justice Roberts rejected this argument, saying the law "does not classify on the basis of transgender status."[17]

As a result, Roberts said that the Court did not need to decide what level of scrutiny should be used for discrimination based on gender identity.

In justifying the majority's conclusion, the court relied on *Geduldig v. Aiello*, which held that excluding pregnancy, and only pregnancy, from disability coverage was not sex discrimination.[18] In that case, the Court reasoned that there were two categories of people—non-pregnant persons and pregnant persons—and because women are in both categories, discrimination based on pregnancy is not sex discrimination. As Justice Ruth Bader Ginsburg later remarked, *Geduldig* was "egregiously wrong": "pregnancy discrimination is inevitably sex discrimination."[19]

Chief Justice Roberts said that there are two groups: those who would use the hormonal treatment for gender-affirming care, which is prohibited by the Tennessee law, and those who would use the hormonal treatment for other purposes, which is allowed. He said that since transgender individuals are in both groups, there is no discrimination against them.

Justice Sotomayor, in her dissent, said that is exactly what the law does: It singles out transgender youth and bars them from receiving certain medical care. She stressed that the entire purpose of the law is prohibiting medical treatments that transgender youth, their parents, and their doctors believe is appropriate. Justice Sotomayor said that the approach also leads to absurd conclusions. She said that that the Court's approach would mean that "a law depriving all individuals who 'have ever, or may someday, menstruate' of access to health insurance would be sex neutral merely because not all women menstruate."[20]

By concluding that rational basis review is appropriate, the Court justified deference to the Tennessee legislature. Chief Justice Roberts wrote:

> *The rational basis inquiry employs a relatively relaxed standard reflecting the Court's awareness that the drawing of lines that create distinctions is peculiarly a legislative task and an unavoidable one. Under this standard, we will uphold a statutory classification so long as there is any reasonably conceivable state of facts that could provide a rational basis for the classification. Where there exist plausible reasons for the relevant government action, our inquiry is at an end.*[21]

The Court then concluded that "SB1 clearly meets this standard."[22]

Justice Sotomayor strongly disagreed, arguing that intermediate scrutiny is appropriate and that the law fails this review. She wrote of the enormous human costs of upholding state laws prohibiting gender-affirming care. She noted, "Tragically, studies suggest that as many as one-third of transgender high school students attempt suicide in any given year."[23] She added: "By retreating from meaningful judicial review exactly where it matters most, the Court abandons transgender children and their families to political whims."[24]

There were three concurring opinions. Each of the concurring justices—Thomas, Alito, and Barrett—reached the issue the majority did not decide: What level of scrutiny should be used for laws discriminating based on gender identity. All three justices said only rational basis review is appropriate. Justice Barrett, for example, wrote:

> *In my view, transgender status does not qualify under our precedents as a suspect or "quasi-suspect" class. Transgender status is not "immutable," and as a result, persons can and do move into and out of the class. Members of the class differ widely among themselves, and it is often difficult for others to determine whether a person is a member of the class. And transgender individuals have not been subjected to a history of discrimination that is comparable to past discrimination against the groups we have classified as suspect or "quasi-suspect."*[25]

Implications

The case, of course, means that state laws prohibiting gender-affirming care to transgender youth do not violate equal protection. It is important to note that the Court did not address whether the state laws might be challenged on another ground: that they violate the right of parents to control the upbringing of their children. This issue was not before the Court and remains open for litigation.

The implications of the decision, though, extend beyond the prohibitions in Tennessee and other states against gender-affirming care for transgender youth. The Trump administration has barred transgender individuals from serving in the military.[26] It also aggressively seeks to end federal support for gender-affirming care for all patients, regardless of age.[27] There are laws that require that individuals play on the athletic teams that correspond to their birth sex and that regulate what restrooms a person can use.[28]

The Supreme Court's *Skrmetti* decision suggests its willingness to defer to legislatures and uphold such government actions discriminating based on gender identity. In fact, in an earlier 6–3 ruling, the Supreme Court lifted a preliminary injunction barring President Trump's executive order barring transgender individuals from serving in the military.[29] Though none of the justices wrote an opinion, it clearly indicated the Roberts Court's deference to the government and lack of receptivity to claims of discrimination against transgender individuals.

The justices sharply disagree about how discrimination against transgender individuals should be handled under equal protection. The dissenters see a history of discrimination against a politically vulnerable minority and want judicial protection. But the justices in the majority see no need for heightened scrutiny and likely will leave protection of transgender individuals to the political process.

Endnotes

1. 145 S. Ct. 1816 (2025).
2. *Map: Attacks on Gender Affirming Care by State*, HRC Foundation, https://www.hrc.org/resources/attacks-on-gender-affirming-care-by-state-map (last visited Aug. 13, 2025).
3. *Id.*
4. *Id.*
5. Tenn. Code Ann. § 68-33-101 (n) (Supp. 2023).
6. *Id.* § 68-33-102 (6).
7. L.W. v. Skrmetti, 679 F. Supp. 3d 668, 715 (M.D. Tenn. 2023).
8. *Id.* at 708–09.
9. *Id.* at 708.
10. L.W. v. Skrmetti, 83 F.4th 460, 491 (6th Cir. 2023).
11. *Id.* at 480.
12. United States v. Skrmetti, 145 S. Ct. 1816, 1837 (2025).

13. *Id.* at 1849 (Thomas, J., concurring).
14. *Id.* at 1829.
15. *Id.* at 1873 (Sotomayor, J., dissenting).
16. 590 U.S. 644 (2020).
17. *Skrmetti*, 145 S. Ct. at 1833.
18. 417 U.S. 484 (1974).
19. Coleman v. Ct. of App. of Md., 566 U.S. 30, 56–57 (2012) (Ginsburg, J., dissenting).
20. 145 S. Ct. at 1880 (Sotomayor, J., dissenting).
21. 145 S. Ct. at 1835.
22. *Id.*
23. *Id.* at 1869 (Sotomayor, J., dissenting).
24. *Id.* at 1868.
25. *Id.* at 1860 (Barrett, J., concurring).
26. Exec. Order No. 14183, 90 Fed. Reg. 8757 (2025).
27. *See* Lindsay Dawson & Jennifer Kates, *Overview of President Trump's Executive Actions Impacting LGBTQ+ Health*, KFF (June 4, 2025), https://www.kff.org/other/fact-sheet/overview-of-president-trumps-executive-actions-impacting-lgbtq-health/.
28. As discussed in Chapter 14, the Supreme Court has granted review in two cases for October Term 2025 as to whether state laws may prevent transgender youth from participating in athletic teams that correspond with their gender identity.
29. App. For Stay, United States v. Shilling, No. 24A1030, 2025 WL 1300282 (May 6, 2025).

Chapter 9

First Amendment: Religion

In recent years, the Roberts Court has dramatically changed the law with regard to the religion clauses of the First Amendment. Again, this term, the Court had several cases about the Constitution and religion.

For decades, in dealing with the establishment clause, the Court saw it as embodying the words of Thomas Jefferson, that there should be a wall separating church and state. Now, though, it is clear that a majority of the justices reject this view. In *Kennedy v. Bremerton School District*, in 2022, the Court said that under the establishment clause, "the line that courts and governments must draw between the permissible and the impermissible has to accor[d] with history and faithfully reflec[t] the understanding of the Founding Fathers."[1] It appears that the Court's approach is that the government violates the establishment clause only if it discriminates among religions or coerces religious behavior, though the Court has not yet provided a definition of what "coercion" means in this context.

At the same time, for several decades, the Court had taken a minimalist approach to the free exercise clause. In *Employment Division v. Smith*, 1990, the Court held that the free exercise clause cannot be used to challenge a general law that was not motivated by a desire to interfere with religion.[2] But in a series of cases over the last decade, the Court has taken a much more robust approach to protecting free exercise of religion, and a majority of the justices have questioned the *Smith* test. For example, the Court has held that it violates free exercise of religion to deny religious schools benefits that are provided to secular private schools.[3] Also, the Court invalidated Covid restrictions applied to religious institutions, concluding that free exercise of religion requires that religion be treated as favorably as the most leniently regulated comparable secular activity.[4]

More generally, in recent years, issues that previously had been regarded as involving the establishment clause have been recast as being about the free exercise clause. For example, for decades the issue was when government aid to religious schools violates the establishment clause. Now, the litigation is about when the failure to provide aid to religious schools infringes free exercise of religion. Similarly, in many cases the Court found that the presence of religion in public schools violates the establishment clause. But cases like *Kennedy v. Bremerton School District* have found that the exclusion of religion infringes the free exercise clause.

This term, there were three religion cases. Two found violations of the First Amendment, and the third was not decided because the Court split 4–4. But it presents an issue—whether the government denying funding to religiously affiliated charter schools violates the free exercise clause—that is sure to return to the Court.

Catholic Charities Bureau, Inc. v. Wisconsin Labor & Industry Review Commission[5]

Wisconsin law provides an exemption from the state's unemployment tax for "an organization operated primarily for religious purposes."[6] Under this exemption, churches, religious schools, and some religious groups do not have to pay the unemployment taxes. Wisconsin denied this exemption to Catholic Charities, a social ministry arm of each Roman Catholic diocese in Wisconsin.

Catholic Charities argues that this violates their free exercise of religion. It says that its mission is to "carry on the redeeming work of our Lord by reflecting gospel values and the moral teaching of the church."[7] In its brief it argues, "Put simply, Wisconsin has taken it upon itself to decide which activities can be religious and which ones can't. That is wrong. Wisconsin courts should not be in the business of deciding religious questions."[8]

The State of Wisconsin, by contrast, in its brief echoed the ruling of the Wisconsin Supreme Court, that the activities of Catholic Charities are secular even though its motivations are religious.[9] Wisconsin emphasizes that Catholic Charities is providing social services to those of all faiths and without any religious content. The state says that if it is forced to expand the religious exemption, it likely would have to eliminate it altogether.

The Supreme Court unanimously ruled in favor of Catholic Charities, with Justice Sonia Sotomayor writing for the Court. She explained that when the government discriminates among religions its action is unconstitutional unless strict scrutiny is met. She wrote, "'The clearest command of the Establishment Clause' is that the government may not 'officially prefe[r]' one religious denomination over another. This principle of denominational neutrality bars States from passing laws that 'aid or oppose' particular religions, or interfere in the 'competition between sects.'"[10] She continued, "To guard against that serious harm, this Court in *Larson v. Valente*, set a demanding standard for the government to justify differential treatment across religions on denominational lines. When a state law establishes a denominational preference, courts must 'treat the law as suspect' and apply 'strict scrutiny in adjudging its constitutionality.' The government bears the burden to show that the relevant law, or application thereof, is 'closely fitted to further a compelling governmental interest.'"[11]

The Court concluded that the Wisconsin law violated the establishment clause because it discriminated among religions. Catholic Charities was denied the exemption under Wisconsin law because it provided social services to those of all religions and because it did not attempt to proselytize or indoctrinate into the faith. But this would mean that religions that engaged in this behavior would receive the tax benefit. That, Justice Sotomayor said, is discrimination among religions: "Much like a law exempting only those religious organizations that perform baptisms or worship on Sundays, an exemption that requires proselytization or exclusive service of co-religionists establishes a preference for certain religions based on the commands of their religious doctrine."[12] She said,

"In short, as applied to petitioners by the Wisconsin Supreme Court, Wis. Stat. § 108.02(15)(h)(2) imposes a denominational preference by differentiating between religions based on theological choices."[13]

The Court concluded that Wisconsin failed to meet strict scrutiny. It rejected the claim that the discrimination was necessary for Wisconsin to maintain its unemployment system. It also said that there was no reason to believe that giving the tax break to Catholic Charities would unduly enmesh the state in religious matters.

For the Court, this seemed to be an easy case. But I wondered how can a state determine what is a "religious purpose," without discriminating among religions? The Supreme Court understandably always has avoided defining religion under the First Amendment. But doesn't any effort to define what is and what isn't a religious purpose risk drawing distinctions among those who claim they are acting for a religious purpose? Indeed, the more the Court gives exemptions to laws for religions, the greater will be the need for it to face the daunting task of trying to define religion.

The case is significant in showing that although the Court has greatly weakened the limits of the establishment clause, it will continue to use strict scrutiny under it when the government discriminates among religions.

Mahmoud v. Taylor[14]

The question presented in *Mahmoud v. Taylor* was "Whether public schools burden parents' religious exercise when they compel elementary school children to participate in instruction on gender and sexuality against their parents' religious convictions and without notice or opportunity to opt out."

In 2022, the Montgomery County School Board approved a group of "LGBTQ-inclusive Books as part of the English Language Arts Curriculum" for use in the Montgomery County Public Schools. These storybooks present gay and lesbian, transgender, and nonbinary characters in various situations. All portray them in favorable lights.

For example, *Intersection Allies* includes Kate, who is apparently a transgender child. The book shows Kate in a sex-neutral or sex-ambiguous bathroom, and Kate proclaims: "My friends defend my choices and place. A bathroom, like all rooms, should be a safe space." *Intersection Allies* includes a "Page-by-Page Book Discussion Guide" that asserts: "When we are born, our gender is often decided for us based on our sex. . . . But at any point in our lives, we can choose to identify with one gender, multiple genders, or neither gender."[15] The discussion guide explains that "Kate prefers the pronouns they/their/them" and asks, "What pronouns fit you best?"[16]

Prince & Knight tells the story of a prince who discovers that he is gay and the whole kingdom later applauds "on the two men's wedding day."[17] Another story, *Love Violet*, shows a young girl who is attracted to another girl.[18] *Born Ready: The True Story of a Boy Named Penelope* tells the story of a transgender boy.[19]

A group of parents brought a challenge contending that it violates free exercise of religion to fail to provide them notice and the opportunity to opt out of having their children read these books. The plaintiffs relied primarily on the Supreme Court's decision in *Wisconsin v. Yoder*, 1972, which held that the free exercise clause prohibits government schools from substantially interfering with the right of parents to direct the religious upbringing of their children. The Court in that case stated: "The conclusion is inescapable that secondary schooling, by exposing Amish children to worldly influences in terms of attitudes, goals, and values contrary to beliefs, and by substantially interfering with the religious development of the Amish child and his integration into the way of life of the Amish faith community at the crucial adolescent stage of development, contravenes the basic religious tenets and practice of the Amish faith, both as to the parent and the child."[20] The Court ruled that Amish parents had the right to exempt their children from compulsory schooling after the eighth grade.

The Supreme Court, in a 6–3 decision, reversed the lower courts and held that parents have a First Amendment right to notice and to have their children opt out of instruction if they believe it would violate their religious beliefs for the children to be exposed to particular material. Justice Samuel Alito wrote the opinion for the Court and applied *Wisconsin v. Yoder*. He said, "'[W]e have long recognized the rights of parents to direct the religious upbringing of their children.' And we have held that those rights are violated by government policies that 'substantially interfer[e] with the religious development' of children."[21]

The issue was whether free exercise of religion was violated by not providing parents notice and the ability to opt out of the curriculum that portrayed gay, lesbian, and transgender individuals in a favorable light. The Court concluded: "In light of the record before us, we hold that the Board's introduction of the LGBTQ+-inclusive storybooks—combined with its decision to withhold notice to parents and to forbid opt outs—substantially interferes with the religious development of their children and imposes the kind of burden on religious exercise that *Yoder* found unacceptable."[22]

Simply put, the Court said that the books portrayed same-sex marriage in a favorable light, but some parents have a different view based on their religious beliefs. Likewise, the books presented gender identity as different from biological sex, and the Court said some parents disagree based on their religious views. Justice Alito wrote:

> *These books carry with them "a very real threat of undermining" the religious beliefs that the parents wish to instill in their children. Like the compulsory high school education considered in* Yoder*, these books impose upon children a set of values and beliefs that are "hostile" to their parents' religious beliefs. And the books exert upon children a psychological "pressure to conform" to their specific viewpoints. The books therefore present the same kind of "objective danger to the free exercise of religion" that we identified in* Yoder*. That "objective danger" is only exacerbated by the fact that the books will be presented to young children by authority figures in elementary school classrooms.*[23]

The Court said that this burdening of religion required that the government meet strict scrutiny. It said that *Wisconsin v. Yoder* is an exception to the usual rule, under *Employment Division v. Smith*, that the free exercise clause cannot be used to gain an exception from general laws.[24] It concluded the school system failed to do so. As a result, the Court concluded that free exercise of religion required that the parents be given notice and the opportunity to opt out of this curriculum.

Justice Sonia Sotomayor wrote a blistering dissent. First, she strongly disagreed with the majority that mere exposure to material is a substantial burdening of free exercise of religion. She said, "[N]ever, in the context of public schools or elsewhere, has this Court held that mere exposure to concepts inconsistent with one's religious beliefs could give rise to a First Amendment claim."[25] She disagreed that *Yoder* supported a First Amendment right for parents to exempt their children from instruction with material with which they have a religious disagreement.

Second, she raised great concerns over what it will mean that parents have the right to notice and opt out of anything they find objectionable on religious grounds. She wrote:

> *The result will be chaos for this Nation's public schools. Requiring schools to provide advance notice and the chance to opt out of every lesson plan or story time that might implicate a parent's religious beliefs will impose impossible administrative burdens on schools. The harm will not be borne by educators alone: Children will suffer too. Classroom disruptions and absences may well inflict long-lasting harm on students' learning and development. Worse yet, the majority closes its eyes to the inevitable chilling effects of its ruling. Many school districts, and particularly the most resource strapped, cannot afford to engage in costly litigation over opt-out rights or to divert resources to tracking and managing student absences. Schools may instead censor their curricula, stripping material that risks generating religious objections. The Court's ruling, in effect, thus hands a subset of parents the right to veto curricular choices long left to locally elected school boards.*[26]

What is striking about Justice Alito's majority opinion is that there is no limiting principle articulated within it. Any time parents believe that exposure to material is inconsistent with their religious beliefs they will have a right to notice and to allow children to opt out. How will school administrators know what some parent might object to? How will they know when to provide notice and to whom? How will schools structure their curriculums with parents having the right to remove their children from particular instruction? For example, some parents surely will object to science courses where evolution is taught. Other parents will object to English classes where there are books like *The Wizard of Oz* or *Harry*

Potter, where there are witches and witchcraft. Yet others will object to books that favorably present mothers working outside the home. And, as this case shows, some surely will object to books that favorably present gays or lesbians or transgender individuals. Will this create pressure for schools to only present material that no parents are likely to claim violates their religion?

Interestingly, Justice Alito's opinion might provide a basis for challenging religion in public schools. At a time when many states are trying to bring the Bible, the Ten Commandments, and religion into public school classrooms, *Mahmoud v. Taylor* can provide a basis for challenging this. The Supreme Court has weakened the protections of the establishment clause, such as in *Kennedy v. Bremerton School*, by saying that what violates that provision is determined by the views of the "founding fathers."[27] But after *Mahmoud v. Taylor*, parents can object that exposure to religious material infringes their free exercise of religion, even if claims under the establishment clause have been made more difficult.

Oklahoma Statewide Charter School Board v. Drummond[28]

In a series of cases over the last eight years, the Supreme Court has held that it violates free exercise of religion for the government to deny benefits to a religious school that it provides to a private secular school. In *Trinity Lutheran v. Comer*, in 2017, the Court held that it was unconstitutional for the State of Missouri to provide aid for surfacing playgrounds to public and secular private schools but not to religious schools.[29] In *Espinoza v. Montana Department of Revenue*, in 2020, the Court ruled that it violated free exercise of religion for Montana to provide a tax credit for those providing assistance to secular private schools but not religious schools.[30] And in *Carson v. Makin*, in 2022, the Court concluded that Maine violated free exercise of religion when it provided funds for children in rural areas without public schools to attend private schools but would not allow the money to be used for religious schools.[31]

After these cases, it was expected that the issue would arise as to whether religious institutions have a First Amendment right to create charter schools. Almost every state has charter schools. These are schools created by state law, funded by the government but run by private entities. Because they have been seen as public schools, state laws require that they be secular.

Oklahoma Statewide Charter School Board v. Drummond involved a challenge by religious schools to the Oklahoma Supreme Court's refusal to allow it to be a charter school.[32] The question presented was "[w]hether Oklahoma violates the First Amendment's guarantee of the free exercise of religion when it excludes privately run religious charter schools from the state's charter-school program because they are religious."[33]

The Oklahoma Statewide Charter School Board, which certifies charter schools in Oklahoma, would have allowed St. Isidore, an online Catholic school operated by the Archdiocese of Oklahoma City and Diocese of Tulsa, to be certified as a charter school. But the Oklahoma Supreme Court ruled that this would violate the Oklahoma Constitution.

Recent Supreme Court decisions have held that the government cannot deny religious schools the benefits it provides secular private schools. But this case goes much further: Does the Constitution require that the government allow religious institutions to create public schools? Would this mean that every religious school could become a public charter school if it wished to do so? Ultimately, the question is what does it mean for a school to be a "public school." Should charter schools be treated as private schools, so that the denial of aid to them violates free exercise of religion? Or because they are created pursuant to state law and funded by the government, should they be treated as public schools for purposes of the First Amendment?

After the oral arguments, the Supreme Court announced that the justices were divided 4–4, and thus the decision of the Oklahoma Supreme Court was affirmed by an evenly divided Court. Justice Amy Coney Barrett was recused. When the justices split 4–4 they do not announce which justices are on which side of the divide. Nor does the recused justice explain the basis for the disqualification.

The issue is sure to return to the Supreme Court. Charter schools exist in almost all states and state laws prohibit them from being religious. When the question comes back to the Court, it seems highly likely that the issue will come down to Justice Barrett's vote.

Endnotes

1. Kennedy v. Bremerton Sch. Dist., 142 S. Ct. 2407, 2428 (2022).
2. Emp. Div., Dep't of Hum. Res. of Or. v. Smith, 110 S. Ct. 1595, 1600 (1990).
3. *See* Carson *ex rel.* O.C. v. Makin, 142 S. Ct. 1987, 1989, 2000 (2022); Espinoza v. Montana Dep't of Revenue, 140 S. Ct. 2246, 2249, 2261 (2020); Trinity Lutheran Church of Columbia, Inc. v. Comer, 137 S. Ct. 2012, 2019 (2017).
4. *See, e.g.*, Tandon v. Newsom, 141 S. Ct. 1294, 1296 (2021).
5. 145 S. Ct. 1583 (2025).
6. Wis. Stat. § 108.02(15)(h)(2).
7. Brief for Petitioners at 6, Catholic Charities Bureau, Inc. v. Wis. Labor & Indus. Rev. Comm'n, No. 24-154 (U.S. Jan. 27, 2025).
8. *Id.* at 38.
9. *See* Brief for Respondents at 1–2, Catholic Charities Bureau, Inc. v. Wis. Labor & Indus. Rev. Comm'n, No. 24-154 (U.S. Feb. 26, 2025).
10. Catholic Charities, 145 S. Ct. at 1591 (citations omitted).
11. *Id.*
12. *Id.* at 1592.
13. *Id.*
14. 145 S. Ct. 2332 (2025).
15. *Id.* at 5.
16. *Id.*
17. *Id.*
18. *Id.*
19. *Id.*
20. Wisconsin v. Yoder, 92 S. Ct. 1526, 1534 (1972).
21. Mahmoud, 145 S. Ct. 2350 (2025).
22. *Id.* at 2353.
23. *Id.* at 2355.
24. *Id.* at 2361 ; *Emp. Div.*, 110 S. Ct. at 1596.
25. Mahmoud, 145 S. Ct. at 2387 (Sotomayor, J., dissenting) (2025).
26. *Id.* at 2.
27. Kennedy v. Bremerton Sch. Dist., 142 S. Ct. 2407, 2428 (2022).
28. 145 S. Ct. 1381 (2025).
29. *See* Trinity Lutheran, 137 S. Ct. at 2024 (2017).
30. *See* Espinoza, 140 S. Ct. at 2261 (2020).
31. *See* Carson, 142 S. Ct. at 1997, 2000, 2002 (2022).
32. *See* Okla. Statewide Charter Sch. Bd., 145 S. Ct. 1381 (2025) (affirming by equally divided Court).
33. Pet. for Writ of Cert. at i, Okla. Statewide Charter Sch. Bd., No. 24-394 (U.S. filed Oct. 7, 2024).

Chapter 10

First Amendment: Speech

The Supreme Court decided two cases concerning freedom of speech in October Term 2024: *TikTok, Inc. v. Garland*[1] and *Free Speech Coalition v. Paxton*.[2] Although they arose in very different contexts, they shared certain characteristics. In both, the Supreme Court found that they were content neutral laws and therefore intermediate scrutiny is the appropriate test. And in both, the Court gave deference to the government and upheld the laws.

TikTok, Inc. v. Garland

The Supreme Court's decision on January 17, 2025, upholding the constitutionality of the federal law banning TikTok, continues a long history of judicial deference to government claims of national security. The ruling upholds a federal statute that bans a medium of communication that is used by more than 170 million people in the United States. The speech of all who generate content for it and all who receive it is restricted by this law. It is difficult to think of any law in American history that restricted so much speech for so many people.

TikTok stopped operating in the United States for a brief time after the Court's decision. Upon taking office, President Donald Trump issued an executive order delaying the TikTok ban from going into effect for 75 days.[3] He has no authority to do this under the federal statute. The law allows the President to extend the time for the TikTok ban to go into effect only if there is substantial progress toward a sale, and none has been suggested. Subsequently, President Trump has repeatedly extended his suspension of the law.[4] Attorney General Pam Bondi has told companies that the government will not be enforcing the federal law. Since no court has enjoined President Trump's order, TikTok at least has a temporary reprieve. The ultimate fate of TikTok in the United States remains uncertain, but for now there is no indication that the Trump administration will take actions to enforce the statute.

On April 24, 2024, President Joe Biden signed the Protecting Americans from Foreign Adversary Controlled Applications Act into law. The act identifies the People's Republic of China and three other countries as foreign adversaries of the United States and prohibits the distribution or maintenance of "foreign adversary controlled applications."[5] The law prohibits TikTok in the United States as of January 19, 2025, unless its owner, ByteDance Ltd., sells it by then.

Under the law, as mentioned, the President may grant a 90-day extension if there is significant progress being made toward a sale of TikTok. ByteDance Ltd. has given no indication that it is interested in a sale, so it is difficult to see President Trump's action fitting within this statutory authority.

On December 6, 2024, the U.S. Court of Appeals for the District of Columbia Circuit upheld the federal law outlawing TikTok.[6] The judges acknowledged the impact of the law on freedom of speech, but they accepted the government's argument that national security concerns justified the ban.

First, the court said that China, through TikTok, could gather information about those in the United States. Second, the Court said that China could attempt to use TikTok to influence attitudes, including about politics, in this country.

The Supreme Court granted certiorari and scheduled oral argument for Friday, January 10. A week later, on January 17, the Court unanimously affirmed the D.C. Circuit in a per curiam opinion.

At the outset, the Supreme Court said that there was the question of whether "heightened review" was appropriate when there was a regulation of non-expressive activity (ownership of a platform) that disproportionately burdens those engaged in expressive activity (those who post on TikTok and receive information there). The Court did not resolve that issue, instead declaring, "We assume without deciding that the challenged provisions fall within this category and are subject to First Amendment scrutiny."[7]

The Court began by reciting the familiar principle that content-based regulations must meet strict scrutiny, while content-neutral laws only need meet intermediate scrutiny. Under strict scrutiny a law must be necessary to achieve a compelling purpose, while under intermediate scrutiny a law need only be substantially related to an important purpose. A law is deemed content based if either it restricts speech based on its topic or its viewpoint.

The Court said that "[a]s applied to petitioners, the challenged provisions are facially content neutral and are justified by a content-neutral rationale."[8] The Court explained that the federal statute was content neutral because it prohibited all speech over TikTok in the United States, whatever its topic and whatever its viewpoint.

The Court identified the government's purpose as preventing China, a foreign adversary, from gathering large amounts of information on Americans using the platform. And it expressly declared that this was a sufficiently important interest to meet intermediate scrutiny: "The Act's prohibitions and divestiture requirement are designed to prevent China—a designated foreign adversary—from leveraging its control over ByteDance Ltd. to capture the personal data of U.S. TikTok users. This objective qualifies as an important Government interest under intermediate scrutiny."[9]

The Court said that China could gather vast amounts of information about users of TikTok, which could include enabling "China to track the locations of Federal employees and contractors, build dossiers of personal information for blackmail, and conduct corporate espionage."[10] The Court stressed that the case arose in the context of "national security and foreign policy" and therefore concluded that "we must accord substantial deference to the predictive judgments of Congress."[11]

Notably, the Court did not echo the D.C. Circuit's conclusion that the TikTok ban was justified because China might use it to influence attitudes in the United States. The premise of the First Amendment is that more speech is inherently better regardless of its source. Restricting speech because it might change minds is antithetical to the First Amendment. Even during the height of the Cold War, the United States allowed the Russian newspaper Pravda to be sold in this country.

The challengers argued that the purpose of the federal law was to prevent TikTok from being used to convey particular views. The Court acknowledged that no prior cases had determined "the appropriate level of First Amendment scrutiny for an Act of Congress justified on both content-neutral and content-based grounds."[12] The Court said that it did not need to decide that issue, but then effectively did by declaring: "The record before us adequately supports the conclusion that Congress would have passed the challenged provisions based on the data collection justification alone."[13] This is an important clarification of First Amendment law: If a government action is justified by both content-based and content-neutral rationales, it will be treated as content neutral so long as the Court is convinced that the law would have been adopted anyway based on the content-neutral rationale.

Justice Sotomayor concurred in part and concurred in the judgment. She agreed with the decision, but said that the Court should have held, not just assumed, that the ban on TikTok was a restriction on expressive activity. She said, "TikTok engages in expressive activity by 'compiling and curating' material on its platform."[14]

Justice Neil Gorsuch concurred in the judgment. He questioned whether the law was actually content neutral, but said it was constitutional under any level of scrutiny. He wrote: "I am persuaded that the law before us seeks to serve a compelling interest: preventing a foreign country, designated by Congress and the President as an adversary of our Nation, from harvesting vast troves of personal information about tens of millions of Americans."[15]

No one in the litigation disputed that TikTok can gain a great deal of information about users of its platform. Nor was it disputed that this information potentially could be obtained by China. What is missing in the Court's analysis is a discussion of what information China can obtain and how that information can be used to damage national security. It is certainly true that every application allows those administering it to gather information about users. But knowing how many people are watching a dance video hardly seems a basis for concluding that national security is endangered. Because the federal law is a very significant restriction on speech there must be a real, proven danger, not conjecture. Yet, the Court did little more than offer a conclusion accepting the government's national security claim.

None of the briefs elaborate this either. Nor is it the case that the Court relied on secret information provided by the government to justify the law. Justice Gorsuch observed: "I am pleased that the Court declines to consider the classified evidence the government has submitted to us but shielded from petitioners and their counsel."[16]

The Court should have explained in much greater detail what information China could gain from TikTok users and how China possessing this information could harm the United States.

Ultimately then, what explains the Court's conclusion is not a proven likely harm to national security from TikTok. Rather, it is the Court giving deference to the government's claim that TikTok is a threat to national security. There have been many cases throughout American history where the Court has professed such deference. But the crucial question is whether such deference is appropriate when it involves a major restriction on the exercise of a fundamental right.

For now, though, the Court's decision has no effect. It is an unusual, maybe unprecedented situation, where a law was adopted and unanimously upheld by the Supreme Court, but the President immediately said that it would not go into effect. And at least during the Trump presidency, there is no indication that the law ever will be implemented. Even for those who disagree with the law and question its constitutionality, it should be troubling to see the President, without any legal authority, nullifying a federal law.

Free Speech Coalition v. Paxton

A Texas law, H.B. 1181, requires that websites where more than one-third of the content is sexually explicit do age verification. In a 6–3 decision, split along ideological lines, the Court upheld the Texas statute. Justice

Clarence Thomas wrote the opinion for the Court and Justice Elena Kagan wrote for the dissenters.

This, of course, is not the first time the Court has dealt with age verification requirements. In *Ginsberg v. New York*, in 1968, the Court upheld a law that prohibited the sale to minors under age 17 "of material defined to be obscene on the basis of its appeal to them, whether or not it would be obscene to adults."[17] The Court described the case as involving "girlie picture magazines" and stressed the State's "independent interest in the well-being of its youth."[18]

In two subsequent cases, the Court rejected laws restricting access to sexual material over the internet. In *Reno v. American Civil Liberties Union*, the Supreme Court first considered the internet and invalidated key provisions of the Communications Decency Act of 1996.[19] The law made it a federal crime to transmit obscene or indecent material over the internet in a manner likely to be accessible to a minor. Specifically, section 223(a) of the act prohibited the knowing transmission of obscene or indecent messages to any recipient under 18 years of age. A second provision, section 223(d), prohibited the knowing, sending, or displaying of patently offensive messages in a manner that is available to a person under 18 years of age. There were two important affirmative defenses provided for under the law. One covers those who take "good faith, reasonable, effective, and appropriate actions" to restrict access by minors to the prohibited communications. The other covers those who restrict access to covered material by requiring certain designated forms of age proof, such as a verified credit card or an adult identification number or code.

The Supreme Court, in a 7–2 decision, declared the prohibition of indecent material over the internet unconstitutional. The Court recognized that the government has a compelling interest in protecting children from exposure to sexual material, but it said that the government cannot restrict speech available to adults so as to safeguard children.

In *Ashcroft v. American Civil Liberties Union,* the Court returned to the issue of government regulation of sexual speech over the internet and considered the constitutionality of the Child Online Protection Act, which seeks to protect children from exposure to sexual material on the internet.[20] After *Reno v. ACLU* invalidated key provisions of the Communications Decency Act, Congress passed the Child Online Protection

Act, which required that operators of commercial websites restrict access by children to material that the average person "applying contemporary community standards" would find is designed to pander to the minors' prurient interest.[21] This law was different from the Communications Decency Act in that it applied only to commercial websites and it defined the objectionable material in terms of what would be offensive under community standards. The law required that such websites take actions to exclude children, such as by requiring credit cards or age verification services. Thus, perhaps most important, the act was different from its predecessor because it did not prohibit material so long as the commercial website takes the necessary steps to exclude children.

Nonetheless, the federal district court issued a preliminary injunction and ultimately the U.S. Supreme Court affirmed, concluding that there was a substantial likelihood that the law would be declared unconstitutional. Justice Kennedy said that the law was a content-based restriction, since it applied only to sexual content over the internet, and thus must meet strict scrutiny.[22]

Although the Court accepted the government's goal of protecting children from exposure to sexual material as a compelling interest, the Court found that the law was likely unconstitutional because it was not the least restrictive alternative. The Court said that filters, installed by parents, were more likely to be effective than the federal statute. The Court noted that 40 percent of sexual material on the internet comes from overseas and thus would not be regulated by the act, but could be blocked by filters. Moreover, the Court noted that "filters also may be more effective because they can be applied to all forms of Internet communication, including e-mail, not just communications available via the World Wide Web."[23]

But in *Free Speech Coalition v. Paxton*, the Supreme Court came to the opposite conclusion and upheld the Texas law. The Court said, based on *Ginsberg v. New York*, that there is a category of speech of "obscene for minors," even though the expression would not meet the requirements for obscenity which is unprotected by the First Amendment. Justice Thomas wrote: "In sum, two basic principles govern legislation aimed at shielding children from sexually explicit content. A State may not prohibit adults from accessing content that is obscene only to minors. But, it may enact laws to prevent minors from accessing such content."[24]

The crucial issue in the case concerned the level of scrutiny to be used. If it were strict scrutiny, as the challengers argued, then the government would have to use the least restrictive alternative. The law likely would have been declared unconstitutional, for the same reasons that the Child Online Protection Act was struck down in *Ashcroft v. ACLU*. But if it were rational basis review, as the U.S. Court of Appeals for the Fifth Circuit ruled in this case, or intermediate scrutiny, then the government would not have to show that it was using the least restrictive alternative. Since all of the justices agreed that the state had a sufficient interest in protecting children from exposure to sexually explicit material, the case turned on whether strict scrutiny and least restrictive alternative analysis was the appropriate test.

Justice Thomas, writing for the Court, expressly rejected strict scrutiny. In part, he said this was because of the government's interest in protecting children and because he saw the Texas law as having only an incidental effect on speech. He wrote: "Applying our precedents, we hold that intermediate scrutiny applies. H.B. 1181 is an exercise of Texas's traditional power to prevent minors from accessing speech that is obscene from their perspective. To the extent that it burdens adults' rights to access such speech, it has 'only an incidental effect on protected speech,' making it subject to intermediate scrutiny."[25] He declared: "Any burden experienced by adults is therefore only incidental to the statute's regulation of activity that is not protected by the First Amendment. That fact makes intermediate scrutiny the appropriate standard under our precedents."[26]

Justice Thomas stressed that strict scrutiny is a very difficult test to meet and that a law like the Texas statute would likely fail. He explained the importance of upholding such a statute by pointing to how the internet and access to it had changed since *Reno v. ACLU* and *Ashcroft v. ACLU*. He wrote:

> *[I]n 2024, 95 percent of American teens had access to a smartphone, allowing many to access the internet at almost any time and place. Ninety-three percent of teens reported using the internet several times per day, and watching videos is among their most common activities online. The content easily accessible to adolescents online includes massive libraries*

> *of pornographic videos. For instance, in 2019, Pornhub, one of the websites involved in this case, published 1.36 million hours—or over 150 years—of new content. Many of these readily accessible videos portray men raping and physically assaulting women—a far cry from the still images that made up the bulk of online pornography in the 1990s.*[27]

Justice Thomas said that the appropriate test is intermediate scrutiny—the government action had to be substantially related to an important government interest—and concluded that the government met this burden. He concluded his opinion: "H.B. 1181 simply requires adults to verify their age before they can access speech that is obscene to children. It is therefore subject only to intermediate scrutiny, which it readily survives. The statute advances the State's important interest in shielding children from sexually explicit content. And, it is appropriately tailored because it permits users to verify their ages through the established methods of providing government-issued identification and sharing transactional data."[28]

Justice Kagan wrote for the dissenters and emphasized that the Court erred by not using strict scrutiny. She explained that it is well established that strict scrutiny is used for content-based restrictions on speech and that the Texas law was obviously content based: It applied to websites based on their sexual content. She wrote: "Under ordinary First Amendment doctrine, this Court should subject H.B. 1181 to strict scrutiny. That is because H.B. 1181 covers speech constitutionally protected for adults; impedes adults' ability to view that speech; and imposes that burden based on the speech's content. Case closed. And making the right answer yet more obvious, we have said as much four times before, when reviewing statutes imposing similar content-based burdens on protected sexually explicit speech. So the case is closed even tighter: The standard should be strict scrutiny."[29]

She argued that the prior cases establish that there cannot be a restriction on speech available to adults to protect children. Under strict scrutiny, the government must use the least restrictive alternative, and Justice Kagan argued that is the burden that Texas should have to meet for the law to be upheld. She concluded her dissent:

> *I would demand Texas show more, to ensure it is not under-valuing the interest in free expression. Texas can of course take measures to prevent minors from viewing obscene-for-children speech. But if a scheme other than H. B. 1181 can just as well accomplish that objective and better protect adults' First Amendment freedoms, then Texas should have to adopt it (or at least demonstrate some good reason not to). . . . [T]he First Amendment protects those sexually explicit materials, for every adult. So a State cannot target that expression, as Texas has here, any more than is necessary to prevent it from reaching children. That is what we have held in cases indistinguishable from this one. And that is what foundational First Amendment principles demand."*[30]

What are the implications of the decision for First Amendment law? First, the Court seems to create a new category of speech: "obscene for minors." The Court does not define this category, and it seems to indicate that it is speech protected by the First Amendment, but restrictions to protect minors should be seen as incidental restrictions on speech that only have to meet intermediate scrutiny. This is a significant change in the law. It is unclear how to reconcile this decision with *Ashcroft v. ACLU*, other than the Court's sense that the content of the internet is different now than it was earlier. But this would seem to open the door to much greater regulation of sexual speech with the goal of protecting minors.

Second, the issue of what is a content-based restriction on speech, as opposed to an incidental burdening of speech, is crucial in First Amendment analysis in many contexts. The Court deems the Texas law "incidental" and therefore not content based, but does so with relatively little explanation. This, too, could open the door to courts allowing much more government regulation of speech.

Third, there is the question of how much courts should be concerned about chilling access to speech. The challenger argued that adults will refrain from accessing material if they have to provide identification. Justice Thomas' majority opinion brushes this concern aside, but it is emphasized in Justice Kagan's dissent.

Many states are adopting other restrictions on minors' access to social media. Some are preventing minors from having any access to social media without parental consent. The outcome to these cases, too, is likely to turn on the level of scrutiny used by the justices.

Endnotes

1. TikTok Inc. v. Garland, 145 S. Ct. 57 (2025).
2. 145 S. Ct. 2291 (2025).
3. Exec. Order No. 14310, 3 C.F.R. 26913 (2025).
4. Exec. Order No. 14166, 3 C.F.R. 8611 (2025); Exec. Order No. 14258, 3 C.F.R. 15209 (2025).
5. 15 U.S.C. § 9901.
6. TikTok Inc. v. Garland, 122 F.4th 930 (2024).
7. 145 S. Ct. at 66.
8. *Id.* at 67.
9. *Id.* at 69.
10. *Id.*
11. *Id.* at 69.
12. *Id.* at 72.
13. *Id.*
14. *Id.* at 73 (Sotomayor, J., concurring in part and concurring in the judgment).
15. *Id.* at 74 (Gorsuch, J., concurring in the judgment).
16. *Id.*
17. 390 U.S. 629, 631 (1968).
18. *Id.* at 1277, 1281.
19. 521 U.S. 844 (1997).
20. 542 U.S. 656 (2004).
21. 47 U.S.C. § 609.
22. 542 U.S. at 670.
23. *Id.* at 657.
24. 145 S. Ct. 2304.
25. *Id.* at 2306.
26. *Id.* at 2309.
27. *Id.* at 2314.
28. *Id.* at 2319.
29. *Id.* at 2321 (Kagan, J., dissenting).
30. *Id.* at 2331.

Chapter 11

Guns

In the last few years, the Court has decided important cases with regard to the meaning of the Second Amendment. In *New York State Rifle and Pistol Association v. Bruen* (2022), the Court struck down a New York law requiring that a person show a safety need in order to receive a permit to have a gun in public.[1] The Court said that gun regulations violate the Second Amendment unless they are of a type that existed historically. In *United States v. Rahimi* (2024), the Court upheld a federal law that prohibited those under restraining orders in domestic violence cases from having guns.[2]

This term, the Court decided two cases related to firearms. Neither involved the Second Amendment. One involved a federal regulation of so-called ghost guns, guns that people make from parts. The other concerned a lawsuit by Mexico against gun manufacturers and the application of a federal law that precludes civil suits against them.

Bondi v. VanDerStoks[3]

The Gun Control Act of 1968 (GCA) requires individuals engaged in importing, manufacturing, or dealing in firearms to obtain federal licenses, keep sales records, conduct background checks, and mark products with serial numbers before transferring firearms to private buyers.[4] The act defines "firearm" to include "(A) any weapon . . . which will or is designed to or may readily be converted to expel a projectile by the action of an explosive; (B) the frame or receiver of any such weapon; (C) any firearm muffler or firearm silencer; or (D) any destructive device."[5] These mandates aim to keep guns out of criminals' hands through background checks and aid law enforcement in crime investigation through licensing, recordkeeping, and serialization requirements.

Recent years, however, have witnessed significant changes in how guns are made and sold, with companies today being able to make and sell weapon parts kits that individuals can assemble into functional firearms in their own homes. Sales of these kits have grown "exponentially" and have become very attractive to criminals largely due to how the kits are sold.[6] Some manufacturers and dealers take the position that weapon parts kits do not qualify as "firearms" subject to the GCA. As a result, they say, they are free to sell their products without obtaining a federal license, conducting background checks, maintaining sales records, or marking components with serial numbers.

Police departments around the nation have seen a dramatic increase in these untraceable "ghost guns" (privately made firearms assembled from weapon parts kits) used in crimes, jumping from approximately 1,600 in 2017 to over 19,000 in 2021.[7] For example, a Polymer80's "Buy Build Shoot" kit, which contains all components for a Glock-variant semiautomatic pistol, can be assembled in about 20 minutes using common tools and instructions found in publicly available YouTube videos.[8]

In 2022, the Bureau of Alcohol, Tobacco, Firearms and Explosives (ATF) adopted a new rule designed to combat the proliferation of ghost guns, interpreting subsections (A) and (B) of section 921(a)(3) to extend the GCA to cover weapon parts kits "designed to or may readily be completed, assembled, restored, or otherwise converted to expel a projectile by the action of an explosive" and "partially complete, disassembled, or nonfunctional" frames or receivers.[9] The rule specified that raw materials are not covered until they are "clearly identifiable as an unfinished component part of a weapon."[10]

Before ATF's new rule took effect and ATF could begin efforts to enforce its new rule, various gun manufacturers, at-home gunsmiths, and others filed a facial challenge under the Administrative Procedure Act (APA), arguing that the GCA could not be fairly read to encompass weapon parts kits or unfinished frames/receivers.

The Supreme Court reversed the Fifth Circuit and held that the ATF's rule is not facially inconsistent with the GCA. Justice Gorsuch delivered the opinion for the 7–2 majority, joined by Chief Justice Roberts and Justices Sotomayor, Kagan, Kavanaugh, Barrett, and Jackson. Justices Sotomayor, Kavanaugh, and Jackson each filed concurring opinions. Justices Thomas and Alito each filed dissenting opinions.

The Court declared: "The GCA embraces, and thus permits ATF to regulate, some weapon parts kits and unfinished frames or receivers, including those we have discussed."[11] The Court approached the case as a facial challenge, assuming that the plaintiffs' burden was to demonstrate that the rule is inconsistent with the statute on its face, meaning no set of circumstances exist where it would be valid.

The Court concluded that at least some weapon parts kits satisfy the two requirements of the GCA: (1) a "weapon" must be present and (2) that "weapon" must meet one of three criteria: it must be able to "expel a projectile by the action of an explosive, designed to do so, or susceptible of ready conversion to operate that way."[12] Specifically, the Court held that at least some weapon parts kits qualify as "weapons" that "may readily be converted to expel a projectile by the action of an explosive."[13]

The Court looked at the Polymer80's "Buy Build Shoot" as an example and analyzed whether it meets subsection (A)'s two tests, starting with whether Polymer80's offering qualifies as a "weapon."[14] The Court explained that "weapon" has been understood as "an instrument of offensive or defensive combat . . . [such] as a club, sword, gun, or grenade."[15] Justice Gorsuch wrote that the finished "Buy Build Shoot" kit is an instrument of combat since no one "would confuse the semiautomatic pistol (pictured in the decision) with a tool or a toy."[16] Despite the kit requiring some assembly as sold, the Court reasoned that several considerations persuade it that the kit qualifies as a "weapon."

The Court explained that if Congress wanted to regulate only operable firearms, it could have simply addressed "weapons" that can "expel a projectile by the action of an explosive."[17] Instead, Congress set forth that a "weapon" also qualifies for regulation if it is either "'designed' to accomplish that function" or "capable of being 'readily . . . converted' to do so."[18] The Court stated that the latter provision contemplates that some things "short of fully operable" will qualify as "weapons," making it difficult to see how the easy-to-assemble "Buy Build Shoot" kit might not be among them.[19] To implicate the act, not only must a "weapon" be present, but it must also be, at the minimum, capable of being "readily . . . converted to expel a projectile by the action of an explosive."[20] The Court held that "Buy Build Shoot" kit satisfies that test, too.

The Court noted that just because some kits, like Polymer80's, qualify as "weapons" that "can readily be converted" into working firearms does not mean all do. Weapon parts kits vary widely, and not all come as complete as the "Buy Build Shoot" kit. Some kits may require more time, expertise, or specialized tools to finish, and at some point a kit may be "so incomplete or cumbersome to assemble" that it can no longer fairly be described as a "weapon" capable of "read[y] . . . conver[sion]" into a working firearm.[21] However, while there may be situations where gun kits may not be categorized as a "weapon" capable of ready conversion, the Court explained that this case does not require it to "untangle exactly how far subsection (A) reaches."[22]

The Court next addressed whether ATF's new regulation concerning unfinished frames and receivers, section 478.12(c), is facially inconsistent with the GCA. The Court looked at subsection (B) of section 921(a)(3), which permits the agency to regulate the "frame or receiver of any such weapon," to answer the question. The Court found that the GCA reaches, and permits ATF to regulate, at least some "partially complete" frames or receivers.[23]

There were three concurring opinions. Justice Sotomayor's concurrence addressed concerns about whether the ATF's rule might create uncertainty for regulated entities regarding compliance.[24] She dismissed this worry as unfounded, explaining that firearms dealers, manufacturers, and importers have a long history (over half a century) of complying with the GCA's requirements, such as serial numbers, sales records, and background checks. The new rule, she asserted, simply "confirms what was already clear": the GCA's plain text covers firearm kits and unfinished frames/receivers designed for ready conversion, and it "does not tolerate such evasion" of the law.[25] For manufacturers acting in good faith, the rule should not be a surprise or difficult to follow.

Justice Kavanaugh's concurrence focused primarily on mens rea issues related to the ATF's 2022 rule.[26] He acknowledged that despite the Court's ruling, an individual or business acting in good faith might still have "substantial difficulty determining when weapon parts kits or unfinished frames or receivers qualify as firearms," given that the "line is not entirely clear."[27] However, he emphasized that for GCA violations related to licensing, recordkeeping, or serialization, the statute requires the government to prove "willfulness."[28] This means the government must demonstrate that an individual "knew that his conduct was unlawful," not merely that he knew the facts that made his conduct unlawful, which "should help prevent the Government from unfairly penalizing an individual who is not aware that his conduct violates the law."[29]

Justice Jackson's concurrence emphasized the "straightforward" nature of the case's resolution based on the claim presented.[30] Her view was that the central task was to evaluate the scope of rulemaking authority Congress delegated to the executive branch through the GCA. She stated that the respondents' challenge was solely that portions of the ATF's rule "exceed the agency's statutory authority" under the Administrative Procedure Act. Justice Jackson argued that proper judicial review for "excess-of-authority" claims must focus on the "actual statutory boundaries," not on whether unelected judges would have made the same discretionary choices as the agency.[31] She concluded that when the "statute's boundaries do not foreclose the agency's action," the claim that the agency exceeded its authority "should meet its end."[32] She read the Court's majority opinion as consistent with this principle.

Justices Thomas and Alito each wrote a dissenting opinion. Justice Thomas argued that the government, with the Court's blessing, rewrites statutory text to regulate weapon parts kits, an overreach he would not support.[33] He criticized the majority's "facial challenge" standard as "plainly inapt in a challenge to a regulatory definition."[34] He contends that if a regulatory definition is deemed valid as long as it covers "at least some" items also covered by the statute, it becomes "difficult to understand how an agency would ever promulgate an invalid definition."[35]

He asserted that the ordinary meaning of "weapon" is an "instrument of offensive or defensive combat" and a weapon parts kit is not a weapon until it is converted into an operable gun.[36] Justice Thomas warned that the ATF's logic—that an object "is what it may be converted into"—could lead to semiautomatic AR-15 receivers being classified as "machineguns" under the National Firearms Act (NFA), exposing millions of owners to criminal liability.[37]

Justice Alito's dissent echoed Justice Thomas' concern with analyzing this under the standard for facial constitutional challenges where a law is facially unconstitutional only if there are no conceivable constitutional applications.[38] He questioned whether the *Salerno* test, designed for constitutional challenges to statutes, should apply to challenges to regulations under the APA, arguing it could make it nearly impossible to invalidate regulatory definitions and would be a "huge boon for the administrative state."[39]

This case is important because of its public safety implications. The Supreme Court's decision means that the ATF's rule, interpreting the GCA to cover certain weapon parts kits and unfinished frames/receivers, is not facially invalid, thus allowing the agency to continue efforts to regulate untraceable "ghost guns." None of the justices questioned the government's interest in regulating ghost guns. But the ruling is also narrow, resolving only the facial challenge and not addressing potential "as-applied" challenges to specific products or the ATF's regulatory authority, leaving those questions for another day.

This case also raises an important issue—which is the primary disagreement between the majority and the dissent—that is, what should be the standard for determining a facial challenge to a regulation under the Administrative Procedures Act. The majority opinion applies the test from *United States v. Salerno*: A regulation is facially invalid only if there are no conceivable permissible applications.[40] The dissent, though, disagrees that the *Salerno* test is appropriate in deciding challenges to agency actions under the Administrative Procedures Act.

Smith & Wesson Brands, Inc. v. Estados Unidos Mexicanos[41]

The Protection of Lawful Commerce in Arms Act (PLCAA) bars certain lawsuits against firearms manufacturers and sellers for harms stemming from the criminal or unlawful misuse of a firearm by a third party. However, PLCAA has a "predicate exception" that allows lawsuits to proceed if the defendant manufacturer or seller "knowingly violated a State or Federal statute applicable to the sale or marketing" of firearms, and that "violation was a proximate cause of the harm."[42] The predicate exception itself lists as examples two ways in which aiding and abetting qualifies: (1) when a gun manufacturer (or seller) "aids and abets" another person either in making "a false statement about a gun sale's legality or in making specified criminal sales"; and (2) more broadly, "aiding and abetting" can qualify as a PLCAA predicate violation "by virtue of another law assimilating an accomplice's liability to a principal's."[43]

A gun manufacturer that aids and abets a federal gun crime may itself commit a PLCAA predicate violation. The government of Mexico sued seven American gun manufacturers, alleging they aided and abetted unlawful gun sales that routed firearms to Mexican drug cartels. Mexico's basic theory was that the defendants failed to exercise "reasonable care" to prevent trafficking of their guns into Mexico, making them responsible for the resulting harms.

The complaint alleged that PLCAA's predicate exception was met by asserting the manufacturers were "willful accessories" in unlawful gun sales by retail dealers, which in turn enabled Mexican criminals to acquire guns. Mexico's allegations regarding how the manufacturers aided and abetted included three main points: (1) supplying firearms to retail dealers whom they knew illegally sold to Mexican gun traffickers; (2) failing to impose controls on their distribution networks to prevent illegal sales to Mexican traffickers; and (3) making "design and marketing decisions" intended to stimulate cartel members' demand for their products.

The District Court dismissed the complaint, but the U.S. Court of Appeals for the First Circuit reversed, finding Mexico had plausibly alleged that defendants aided and abetted illegal firearms sales.[44] The First Circuit found that the exception within PLCAA for suits against gun manufacturers was met.

The Supreme Court unanimously reversed and held that PLCAA bars the lawsuit because Mexico's complaint does not plausibly allege that the defendant gun manufacturers aided and abetted gun dealers' unlawful sales of firearms to Mexican traffickers.

Justice Elena Kagan wrote for the Court and explained that the Court "need not address the proximate cause question," because it found that

Mexico had not "plausibly alleged aiding and abetting on the manufacturers' part."[45] Justice Kagan explained federal aiding and abetting law requires a person to take an affirmative act in furtherance of the offense and intend to facilitate its commission. She said that according to Learned Hand, this means that an "aider and abettor" must participate in a crime "as in something that he wishes to bring about" and seeking "by his action to make it succeed."[46]

The Court rejected Mexico's claim that manufacturers sell to known rogue dealers failed for a "package of reasons."[47] The Court said that "it is far from clear" that such behavior by the gun manufacturers, without more, "could ever count as aiding and abetting under our precedents."[48] The Court also rejected Mexico's allegations that manufacturers failed to impose controls on distribution networks. Justice Kagan explained that "passive nonfeasance" or "omissions" are rarely sufficient for aiding-and-abetting liability, especially in an already highly regulated industry.[49] The Court held that a "manufacturer of goods is not an accomplice to every unaffiliated retailer whom it fails to make follow the law."[50]

The Court concluded that the predicate exception of the PLCAA allows for accomplice liability only when "a plaintiff makes a plausible allegation" that a gun manufacturer "'participate[d] in' a firearms violation 'as in something that [it] wishe[d] to bring about' and sought to make succeed."[51] The Court concluded that because Mexico's complaint fails to do so, the defendant manufacturers retain their PLCAA-granted immunity.[52]

The decision reaffirms broad immunity for gun manufacturers under PLCAA, even in cases involving foreign governments and cross-border harm. Additionally, the case clarifies the threshold for aiding and abetting liability in gun trafficking cases. The Court made clear PLCAA's "predicate exception" (allowing suits for knowing statutory violations) does not broadly undermine the act's general immunity for gun companies.

Endnotes

1. 142 S. Ct. 2111 (2022).
2. 144 S. Ct. 1889 (2024).
3. 145 S. Ct. 857 (2025).
4. 18 U.S.C. § 921.

5. *Id.* at (a)(3)(A–D).
6. 145 S. Ct. at 860.
7. *Id.* at 864–65.
8. *Id.* at 866.
9. *Id.* at 864.
10. *Id.*
11. *Id.* at 876.
12. *Id.* at 864.
13. *Id.*
14. *Id.* at 867.
15. *Id.*
16. *Id.* at 868.
17. *Id.*
18. *Id.* at 869.
19. *Id.*
20. *Id.*
21. *Id.*
22. *Id.*
23. *Id.* at 872.
24. *Id.* at 876 (Sotomayor, J., concurring).
25. *Id.*
26. *Id.* at 877 (Kavanaugh, J., concurring).
27. *Id.*
28. *Id.*
29. *Id.*
30. *Id.* at 878 (Jackson, J., concurring).
31. *Id.*
32. *Id.*
33. *Id.* at 878 (Thomas, J., dissenting).
34. *Id.* at 881.
35. *Id.* at 881, 882.
36. *Id.* at 888.
37. *Id.* at 891.
38. *Id.* at 892 (Alito, J., dissenting).
39. *Id.* at 894.
40. 143 S. Ct. 189 (2022).
41. 145 S. Ct. 1556 (2025).
42. 15 U.S.C. § 7903(5)(A)(iii).
43. 145 S. Ct. at 1562, 1563.
44. 91 F.4th 511, 538 (2024).
45. 145 S. Ct. at 1565.

46. *Id.*
47. *Id.*
48. *Id.* at 1567.
49. *Id.* at 1569.
50. *Id.*
51. *Id.* at 1570.
52. Justice Thomas and Justice Jackson each wrote concurring opinions.

Chapter 12

Immigration Law

As is true every year, the Court decided several cases concerning federal immigration law. This term, none involved constitutional questions. Each involved interpreting the federal immigration statutes as to issues that frequently arise. In light of the Trump administration's much greater focus on deportations, issues of immigration law are likely to play an even larger role in the Court's docket in the years to come.

Bouarfa v. Mayorkas[1]

May federal courts review discretionary actions of the Attorney General or the Secretary of the Department of Homeland Security to revoke a noncitizen's ability to stay in the United States? The Supreme Court in unanimous decision, with the majority opinion written by Justice Ketanji Brown Jackson, said no.

Amina Bouarfa, a U.S. citizen, sought adjustment of status on behalf of her noncitizen spouse, Ala'a Hamayel, under the Immigration and Nationality Act (INA). Bouarfa's petition to classify Hamayel as her immediate relative was initially approved by United States Citizenship and Immigration Services (USCIS). However, two years later, Bouarfa received a Notice of Intent to Revoke the approval based on evidence suggesting her husband Hamayel had entered into a previous marriage for the purpose of evading immigration laws, triggering what is referred to as the "sham-marriage bar."

The Secretary's determination of a sham-marriage was based on statements made by Hamayel's ex-wife, which she later recanted, regarding alleged fraud from nearly a decade prior. The Secretary maintained it had the authority to revoke approval based on this under 8 U.S.C. § 1155, which states that the Secretary "may, at any time, for what he deems to be good and sufficient cause, revoke the approval of any [visa] petition." The Board of Immigration Appeals (BIA) affirmed the revocation, reasoning that the initial approval of the petition was in error given prior insincerity.

Bouarfa then brought suit in federal court under the Administrative Procedure Act, challenging the revocation as an "arbitrary and capricious" abuse of discretion that lacked sufficient evidence to support the Secretary's sham-marriage determination. The Secretary responded with a motion to dismiss, asserting that under 8 U.S.C. § 1252(a)(2)(B)(ii), federal courts have no jurisdiction to review discretionary actions taken by the Attorney General or Secretary.

The issue in this case is whether section 1155 granted the Secretary discretionary authority to revoke prior approval of Bouarfa's petition, and whether that discretionary decision fell under section 1252(a)(2)(B)(ii), thus stripping federal courts of jurisdiction to review the agency's action.

In a unanimous decision written by Justice Jackson, the Supreme Court held that the Secretary's revocation under section 1155 was within the agency's discretionary authority and thus not subject to judicial review. The Court stated: "It is clear on the face of § 1155 that the revocation provision is a quintessential grant of discretion to the Secretary. Once again, that provision provides that the Secretary 'may, at any time, for what he deems to be good and sufficient cause, revoke the approval of any [visa] petition.'"[2]

The Court said that the general "presumption" that administrative action is subject to judicial review "may be overcome by clear and convincing evidence of congressional intent to preclude judicial review."[3] The Court found that in this instance the statute was "clear" and thus overcame any presumption for judicial review. The Court concluded: "In § 1155, Congress granted the Secretary broad authority to revoke an approved visa petition 'at any time, for what he deems to be good and sufficient cause.' Such a revocation is thus 'in the discretion of' the agency. Where § 1252(a)(2)(B)(ii) applies, then, it bars judicial review of the Secretary's revocation under § 1155."

The decision is thus an important preclusion of judicial review, including through the Administrative Procedures Act, of some decisions of the Attorney General and the Secretary of Homeland Security to revoke the ability of people to stay in the United States.

Monsalvo Velazquez v. Bondi[4]

This case involved the ability of a federal court of appeals to review the Bureau of Immigration Appeals denial of reconsideration of an immigration matter and how a time limit for review is to be construed.

Hugo Abisai Monsalvo Velazquez was born in Mexico and entered the United States unlawfully in 2005. In 2011, the government initiated proceedings to remove Monsalvo based on his unlawful entry in 2005. While Monsalvo conceded removability, he requested suspension of removal efforts and relief under the Convention Against Torture, claiming he would face persecution if returned to Mexico. As an alternative, Monsalvo sought voluntary departure under section 1229c of the INA.[5]

In 2019, Monsalvo's persecution claim was determined to be without merit, though he was found to be of "good moral character" and eligible for voluntary departure. Because the end of the 60-day departure deadline period happened to fall on a Saturday, the judge specified that Monsalvo's deadline to depart voluntarily would extend to the following Monday.

On October 12, 2021, the BIA affirmed the denial of relief and issued Monsalvo a new 60-day period to depart. The BIA specified that Monsalvo would face serious penalties if he overstayed the deadline, including losing eligibility to most forms of immigration relief for the next ten years. BIA also advised Monsalvo of his right to file a motion to reopen removal proceedings if he believed he had new and previously unavailable evidence that could alter the assessment of his case. If filed before the expiration of the voluntary departure period, the penalties associated with failing to depart would not apply.[6] Choosing to exercise this right, Monsalvo served a motion to reopen on Friday, December 10, 2021, however it was not filed until the following Monday, on December 13, 2021. The BIA, determining that Monsalvo's departure period expired on Saturday, December 11, rejected his motion. Consequently, Monsalvo was determined to have overstayed his deadline and was subject to severe penalties.

Monsalvo then filed a motion to reconsider, arguing that as a matter of law, "days" in section 1229c(b)(2) should be understood to mean that if a deadline falls on a weekend or holiday, the deadline extends to the next business day. Under this reading, Monsalvo's motion to reopen would no longer be considered late and he would no longer be subject to harsh penalties. The Board rejected this argument, denying Monsalvo's motion for reconsideration. Monsalvo then petitioned the Tenth Circuit to review the Board's denial of his motion for reconsideration. The U.S. Court of Appeals for the Tenth Circuit affirmed the BIA's finding that the motion arrived past its deadline, interpreting section 1229c(b)(2) to refer to ordinary, calendar days.

In a 5–4 decision, with the majority opinion written by Justice Gorsuch, the Supreme Court reversed and remanded. Justice Gorsuch was joined in part by Justices Roberts, Sotomayor, Kagan, and Jackson. Regarding jurisdiction, the Court found that the Tenth Circuit was properly authorized to review a "final order of removal" under section 1252(a)(1).[7] As to the question of statutory interpretation, the Court held that under 8 U.S.C. § 1229c(b)(2), a voluntary departure deadline that falls on a weekend or legal holiday extends to the next business day.

Justice Gorsuch explained that in light of the specialized manner in which deadlines are treated in the immigration context, "it is all the more sensible" to interpret this immigration provision the same way.[8] The Court adds that "exactly nothing" indicates an intent by Congress to stray from existing long-standing practice.

The Court stressed the important implications of treating the calculation of deadlines in this way: "Not only does it affect the time one may have to reopen immigration proceedings. As we have seen, it also affects an individual's exposure to detention, removal, and fines, and carries with it serious ramifications for his ability to seek lawful status for years into the future."[9]

There were several dissenting opinions. Justice Thomas disagreed that the Tenth Circuit had jurisdiction to review the BIA's denial. He reasoned that section 1252, which allows for appellate review, is intended to have limited application, not serve as "a vehicle to head off unwanted post removal consequences."[10] Justice Alito, agreeing with Thomas on the lack of jurisdiction, focuses his dissent on the interpretive issue, insisting "days" should be read in its ordinary sense as calendar days.[11] He stressed that "60 days" means "60 days," adding: "It is probable that nearly half of the departure deadlines in such cases will fall on a Saturday, Sunday, or federal holiday. As a result, these individuals will be given a windfall."[12]

Finally, Justice Barrett wrote her own brief dissent, joined by Justice Kavanaugh. Justice Barrett points out that Monsalvo did not actually contest the validity of the BIA decision. Barrett poses the question to the majority: "How can Monsalvo seek judicial review of his final order of removal while conceding that his final order of removal was lawful? He cannot, so the Tenth Circuit lacked jurisdiction."[13]

One interesting aspect of the case concerns terminology. The majority takes care to refer to those in immigration proceedings as "noncitizens" or "individuals," for which the three dissents instead use the term "alien." Alito's dissent includes a footnote attempting to emphasize how "alien" and "noncitizen" are not synonymous, and seemingly encouraging the majority to defer to his chosen terminology.[14] This parallels the political landscape where conservatives use the word "alien," while others regard this as inappropriate and use noncitizen instead.

Riley v. Bondi[15]

Is the 30-day statute of limitation for seeking judicial review of an order of removal to be regarded as jurisdictional? If so, it cannot be waived and can be raised by the decision-maker even if not by the parties. In *Riley v. Bondi*, the Court held that it is not jurisdictional.

Pierre Yassue Nashun Riley, a native citizen of Jamaica, entered the United States at age 16 to live with his father, a U.S. citizen. He arrived in 1995 on a B-2 tourist visa authorizing a six-month stay, however, upon the visa's expiration, he did not leave. Several years later, in 2008, Riley was found guilty of conspiracy to distribute over 1,000 kilograms of marijuana and for possession of a firearm in furtherance of a drug-trafficking crime. He was sentenced to 25 years' imprisonment. In 2021, after serving nearly 15 years of his sentence, Riley was granted compassionate release.[16]

Shortly after his release, on January 26, 2021, the Department of Homeland Security (DHS) issued Riley a final administrative review order directing him to return to Jamaica based on his aggravated felony convictions. Conceding his convictions and consequent removability under section 1228(b), Riley instead sought relief under the Convention Against Torture, which prohibits removing noncitizens to a nation where their torture is likely. Riley attested that if he were to return to Jamaica, he would likely be killed by a drug dealer kingpin who had previously killed members of his family. The immigration judge found Riley's testimony credible and granted deferral of his removal to Jamaica, sending the case to "withholding-only" proceedings (proceedings where the only issue is whether the noncitizen may be removed to his home country). The Department of Homeland Security appealed the decision to the BIA. The BIA vacated the immigration judge's order on May 31, 2022, finding that Riley had not provided sufficient evidence to support relief under the Convention Against Torture.

Three days later, Riley petitioned the Fourth Circuit to review the BIA's decision. Under section 1252(b)(1), a petition for review of a "final order of removal" must be filed within 30 days of that order. The Fourth Circuit dismissed Riley's request for lack of jurisdiction, asserting that Riley had failed to file on time because the 30-day deadline began to run when the final administrative review order was issued on January 26, 2021. Riley sought Supreme Court review, arguing that the 30-day deadline was not jurisdictional and could only start running after the BIA's decision.

The Supreme Court, in an opinion by Justice Alito, held that (1) section 1252(b)(1) is not jurisdictional and that (2) the filing deadline began to run on January 26, 2021, even with ongoing Convention Against Torture proceedings. Justice Alito was joined by Justices Thomas, Kavanaugh, and Barrett in full, and Justices Sotomayor, Kagan, Gorsuch, and Jackson in part.

In holding section 1252(b)(1) not jurisdictional, Justice Alito reasons that the Supreme Court, over the last decades, has held that statutory limitations should be treated as jurisdictional only if Congress "clearly states" that they have jurisdictional consequences.[17] He said that the Court has been "more disciplined" in using the term "jurisdictional."[18] Accordingly, the Court states it "will not categorize a provision as 'jurisdictional' unless the signal is exceedingly strong. And in this case, that demanding requirement is not met."[19] In other words, the time limit for these appeals is not to be treated as jurisdictional.

Justice Sotomayor dissented in part, and was joined by Justices Kagan and Jackson, and in part by Justice Gorsuch. The dissent agrees with the majority that the 30-day deadline is not jurisdictional and that the relevant "order of removal" was the original final administrative removal order. The dissent disagrees, however, with the determination that the 30-day deadline began to run the day of its issuance on January 26, 2021. Justice Sotomayor focuses on finality, reasoning that because an order becomes "final" only when it leaves no further chance for action or change, the Convention Against Torture order appeal and removal order appeal must be tied together. Justice Sotomayor asserts that "when two orders must be consolidated into the same appeal, it follows inescapably that they become final together, as well,"[20] adding that the majority's decision runs counter to *Monsalvo Velázquez*'s holding just months prior that section 1252 authorizes courts to review the final order of removal.

In her conclusion, Justice Sotomayor disagrees strongly with the majority opinion: "Today's holding deals untold damage to basic principles of finality and judicial review. Time will tell whether the Court will extend its illogic beyond politically disfavored noncitizens." Justice Sotomayor added that the decision will cause considerable chaos to the immigration appeals system, labeling it "a rare holding that benefits no one."[21]

Endnotes

1. 145 S. Ct. 24 (2024).
2. *Id.* at 30.
3. *Id.* at 33.
4. 145 S. Ct. 1232 (2025).
5. *Id.* at 1234.
6. *Id.* at 1237.
7. *Id.* at 1239.
8. *Id.* at 1242.
9. *Id.* at 1238.

10. *Id.* at 1250 (Thomas, J., dissenting).
11. *Id.* at 1256 (Alito, J., dissenting).
12. *Id.* at 1255–56.
13. *Id.* at 1261 (Barrett, J., dissenting).
14. *Id.* at 1262 n.2 (Alito, J., dissenting).
15. 145 S. Ct. 2190 (2025).
16. *Id.* at 2196.
17. *Id.* at 2202 (Alito, J., majority), citing Arbaugh v. Y & H Corp., 546 U.S. 500 (2006).
18. *Id.*
19. *Id.* at 2202.
20. *Id.* at 2212 (Sotomayor, J., dissenting).
21. *Id.* at 2219.

Chapter 13

Presidential Power

The first months of Donald Trump's second term as president have been unlike anything in American history, with the issuance of a large number of executive orders, many of which are of dubious constitutionality and legality. As a result, there have been dozens of district court temporary restraining orders and preliminary injunctions. A number of these have already made it to the Supreme Court on its emergency docket.

Overall, as the title of this book reflects, President Trump has prevailed in the Supreme Court in most of these matters. Two important issues are discussed earlier in the book. After President Trump issued an executive order limiting birthright citizenship, several federal district courts issued nationwide injunctions. In *Trump v. CASA*, the Supreme Court, 6–3, ruled that federal courts generally cannot issue such nationwide injunctions.[1] Although this came to the Supreme Court on its emergency docket, the Court asked for briefs and held oral arguments on May 15, 2025. The Court's decision, which was issued on June 27, is discussed in Chapter 4. The Court did not address the constitutionality of the restriction on birthright citizenship and that seems certain to return to the Supreme Court sometime soon.

The issue of the ability of Congress to limit removal of heads of federal agencies is discussed in Chapter 2. In 1935, in *Humphrey's Executor v. United States*, the Supreme Court ruled that Congress may limit presidential removal of members of federal agencies to where there is good cause for firing.[2] President Trump has expressly declared that he will not abide by this decision, as he believes that it impermissibly limits the ability of the president to exercise control over the executive branch of government. He fired Gwynne Wilcox, a commissioner on the National Labor Relations Board, and Cathy Harris, a member of the Merit System Protection Board, even though there were federal laws limiting removal in both instances and there was no claim of cause for firing. On Thursday, May 22, the Supreme Court, in a 6–3 ruling, lifted a lower court's preliminary injunction that prevented the removal of these two officials. In *Trump v. Wilcox*, the six conservative justices, in an unsigned order, explained that its ruling "reflects our judgment that the Government faces greater risk of harm from an order allowing a removed officer to continue exercising the executive power than a wrongfully removed officer faces from being unable to perform her statutory duty."[3] This is discussed in Chapter 2, which focuses on administrative law.

There are a number of other important matters where the Supreme Court has ruled on its emergency docket.

Detentions and Deportations

The Trump administration has invoked the Alien Enemy Act of 1798 to deport individuals to a maximum-security prison in El Salvador. The Alien Enemy Act provides that in the event of a "declared war" or "invasion," the United States can deport males over the age of 14 who are from an enemy nation. Although this law previously had been used only in the War of 1812, World War I, and World War II, the Trump administration has invoked it to deport alleged members of a Venezuelan gang.

On Monday, April 8, in *Trump v. J.G.G.*, the Court ruled, 5–4, that those facing deportation must bring a habeas corpus petition in the federal district where they are being held, but that they must be given notice and a hearing before being deported.[4] Justice Sotomayor and Justice Jackson wrote dissenting opinions. Justice Sotomayor objected to the Court getting involved at all and would have allowed the case to continue in the District of Columbia, arguing that the Court's "decision to intervene in this litigation is as inexplicable as it is dangerous."[5] She wrote: "The Government's conduct in this litigation poses an extraordinary threat to the rule of law. That a majority of this Court now rewards the Government for its behavior with discretionary equitable relief is indefensible. We, as a Nation and a court of law, should be better than this."[6] Similarly, Justice Jackson lamented the Court dealing with this on its shadow docket: "This fly-by-night approach to the work of the Supreme Court is not only misguided. It is also dangerous. . . . With more and more of our most significant rulings taking place in the shadows of our emergency docket, today's Court leaves less and less of a trace. But make no mistake: We are just as wrong now as we have been in the past, with similarly devastating consequences. It just seems we are now less willing to face it."[7]

On April 19, at about 1:00 a.m., in *A.A.R.P. v. Trump*, the Supreme Court issued an order that the "Government is directed not to remove any member of the putative class of detainees from the United States until further order of this Court."[8] It was a 7–2 ruling, with Justice Alito writing a dissent, joined by Justice Thomas. On May 16, the Court, again 7–2, came to the same conclusion and declared, the "Government is enjoined from removing the named plaintiffs or putative class members in this action under the AEA pending order by the Fifth Circuit and disposition of the petition for a writ of certiorari."[9]

But surprisingly, on June 23, the Supreme Court, without writing an opinion, allowed the government to remove individuals to Guatemala and South Sudan. In *Department of Homeland Security v. D.V.D.*, the Supreme Court, by a 6–3 margin, lifted a preliminary injunction that stopped the government from deporting individuals from Venezuela and Cuba to Guatemala and South Sudan.[10]

Federal law is quite specific as to where a person can be deported to. Specifically 8 U.S.C. § 1231(b)(2)(E), which lists where a noncitizen can be taken:

(i) The country from which the alien was admitted to the United States.

(ii) The country in which is located the foreign port from which the alien left for the United States or for a foreign territory contiguous to the United States.

(iii) A country in which the alien resided before the alien entered the country from which the alien entered the United States.
(iv) The country in which the alien was born.
(v) The country that had sovereignty over the alien's birthplace when the alien was born.
(vi) The country in which the alien's birthplace is located when the alien is ordered removed.
(vii) If impracticable, inadvisable, or impossible to remove the alien to each country described in a previous clause of this subparagraph, another country whose government will accept the alien into that country.

It is clear that the final category is meant to be a last resort. Taking people who are from Venezuela and Cuba to a prison in South Sudan—a country where they have no prior connections—seems clearly to violate the law.

Nonetheless, the Supreme Court lifted the preliminary injunction issued by the federal district court. Most stunning, there was no opinion of explanation. It was just an order reversing the lower court. Justice Sotomayor wrote a blistering dissent, joined by Justices Kagan and Jackson. She began her opinion:

> *In matters of life and death, it is best to proceed with caution. In this case, the Government took the opposite approach. It wrongfully deported one plaintiff to Guatemala, even though an Immigration Judge found he was likely to face torture there. Then, in clear violation of a court order, it deported six more to South Sudan, a nation the State Department considers too unsafe for all but its most critical personnel. An attentive District Court's timely intervention only narrowly prevented a third set of unlawful removals to Libya. Rather than allowing our lower court colleagues to manage this high-stakes litigation with the care and attention it plainly requires, this Court now intervenes to grant the Government emergency relief from an order it has repeatedly defied. I cannot join so gross an abuse of the Court's equitable discretion.*[11]

Justice Sotomayor wrote of the government's defying the district court's orders and said that its "unclean hands" should deny it an equitable remedy. She said that the administration and the majority of the Court ignored that these individuals could face torture or death in these countries. She concluded: "Apparently, the Court finds the idea that thousands will suffer violence in farflung locales more palatable than the remote possibility that a District Court exceeded its remedial powers when it ordered the Government to provide notice and process to which the plaintiffs are constitutionally and statutorily entitled. That use of discretion is as incomprehensible as it is inexcusable."[12]

There also is the separate matter of Kilmar Abrego Garcia, a man in Maryland who was removed to a maximum-security prison in El Salvador. A government lawyer admitted that he was deported by mistake. The federal district court ordered the government to "facilitate and effectuate his return."

Before the U.S. Supreme Court, the Solicitor General filed a brief arguing that no federal court has jurisdiction over a person held in a foreign country. It further argued that a court could not order that the President effectuate the return of a person held in a foreign country because that would infringe the President's control over foreign policy. This would mean that the federal government could take anyone—noncitizen or citizen—and move them to a foreign prison and no court could provide redress. When the matter was before the U.S. Court of Appeals for the Fourth Circuit, Judge J. Harvey Wilkinson spoke forcefully about this assertion of unreviewable executive power: "The facts of this case thus present the potential for a disturbing loophole: namely that the government could whisk individuals to foreign prisons in violation of court orders and then contend, invoking its Article II powers, that it is no longer their custodian, and there is nothing that can be done. It takes no small amount of imagination to understand that this is a path of perfect lawlessness, one that courts cannot condone."[13]

On April 10, the Supreme Court ruled in favor of Abrego Garcia and declared: "The order properly requires the Government to 'facilitate' Abrego Garcia's release from custody in El Salvador and to ensure that his case is handled as it would have been had he not been improperly sent to El

Salvador. The intended scope of the term 'effectuate' in the District Court's order is, however, unclear, and may exceed the District Court's authority. The District Court should clarify its directive, with due regard for the deference owed to the Executive Branch in the conduct of foreign affairs."[14]

After further proceedings in the district court, Abrego Garcia was returned to the United States, charged with federal crimes, and is currently being held in custody.

Spending Cuts

The Trump administration has frozen or cut off billions of dollars of federal money. This has been challenged as violating separation of powers for usurping Congress's control over federal spending and also for violating the Impoundment Control Act. Many district courts have issued temporary restraining orders and preliminary injunctions against the cuts in funding.

Three of these cases have made their way to the Supreme Court and the justices' rulings seem inconsistent. On March 5, in *Department of State v. AIDS Vaccine Advocacy Coalition*, the Court, 5–4, ruled that the federal district court has the authority to order the Trump administration to restore funding for the United States Agency for International Development. The short, unsigned order was issued by Chief Justice Roberts and Justices Sotomayor, Kagan, Barrett, and Jackson. Justice Alito wrote a blistering dissent, rejecting the authority of federal courts to order restoring of cutoff funds. His opinion was joined by Justices Thomas, Gorsuch, and Kavanaugh.

But about a month later, on April 5, the Court came to the opposite conclusion in *Department of Education v. California*. A federal district court issued a temporary restraining order against the Department of Education when it cut off $65 million in teacher training grants. Temporary restraining orders are generally not appealable. Nonetheless, the Supreme Court reversed the district court and lifted the temporary restraining order. The majority was comprised of Justices Thomas, Alito, Gorsuch, Kavanaugh, and Barrett. Chief Justice Roberts joined the three liberal justices, Sotomayor, Kagan, and Jackson, in dissent.

Strikingly, the three-page majority opinion does not dispute that the cutoff of funds was unconstitutional and illegal. As Justice Kagan said in a dissent, "Nowhere in its papers does the Government defend the legality of canceling the education grants at issue here." Instead, the majority suggested that the federal government would be harmed by disbursing the money because if it ultimately prevailed in the litigation, it would be unlikely to recoup the funds. The majority also suggested that the appropriate forum for the case would be an action for breach of contract in the federal Court of Claims.

It is not possible to reconcile these two rulings. Only Justice Barrett was in the majority in both, and she did not write an opinion in either case.

On July 14, in *McMahon v. New York*, the Court stayed a district court order that enjoined the firing of most employees at the Department of Education.[15] The Trump administration announced it was eliminating this agency and was accomplishing this by firing its employees. But Congress created the Department of Education and the lower court ruled that it therefore should be for Congress to abolish it. The Supreme Court, without opinion or explanation, stayed the lower court's order, thus allowing the firing of the workers and the dismantling of the agency.

Transgender Individuals in the Military

President Trump, by executive order, barred transgender individuals from continuing to serve in the military. In his inaugural address, Trump declared, "As of today, it will henceforth be the official policy of the United States government that there are only two genders: male and female." He issued an executive order directing Secretary of Defense Pete Hegseth to put into effect a ban on "individuals with gender dysphoria" from serving in the United States military.

Commander Emily Shilling, who has been a naval aviator for nearly two decades, brought a challenge. The U.S. District Court for the Western District of Washington found that the ban violated equal protection and issued a preliminary injunction to keep it from taking effect. The U.S. Court of Appeals for the Ninth Circuit refused to stay the injunction while the appeal is pending.

On Tuesday, May 6, the Supreme Court, in a 6–3 ruling divided along ideological lines, stayed the district court's order while the federal government's appeal is pending. Neither the majority nor the dissent wrote opinions.

Although it is not a ruling on the merits of the case, it likely reflects the majority's views on the issue. Together with the Court's ruling in *United States v. Skrmetti*,[16] which upheld the constitutionality of a law that prohibits gender-affirming care for transgender youth, it indicates a Court unlikely to provide much protection for transgender individuals.

Conclusion

This, of course, is just the beginning of the Supreme Court considering challenges to Trump administration actions. Other matters are pending now and many, many more are in the lower courts and are sure to come to the Supreme Court. The bottom line is that we are in an unprecedented time with regard to the assertion of presidential powers and the first months of the Trump presidency show a Court likely to uphold, not stop, his actions in most instances.

Endnotes

1. 145 S. Ct. 1917 (2025).
2. 55 S. Ct. 869 (1935).
3. 145 S. Ct. 1415, 1415 (2025).
4. 145 S. Ct. 1003 (2025).
5. *Id.* at 1012 (Sotomayor, J., dissenting).
6. *Id.* at 1016.
7. *Id.* at 1017 (Jackson, J., dissenting).
8. 145 S. Ct. 1034, 1034 (2025).
9. 145 S. Ct. 1364, 1370 (2025).
10. 145 S. Ct. 2153 (2025).
11. *Id.* (Sotomayor, J., dissenting).
12. *Id.* at 2163.
13. Abrego Garcia v. Noem, 145 S. Ct. 1017 (2025).
14. *Id.* at 1018.
15. 145 S. Ct. 2643 (2025).
16. 145 S. Ct. 1816 (2025).

Chapter 14

Looking Ahead

Traditionally, the Court finishes its term by the end of June. There always are a flurry of decisions on the last days, some additional grants of certiorari are announced, and then the justices go off for the summer. The Court usually has been quiet until the beginning of the new term on the first Monday in October. But this has changed as the Court's emergency docket has grown. And with the dramatic increase in emergency matters coming before the Court during the first months of the Trump presidency, has meant that the justices have been very active during the summer of 2025. Officially, these rulings will be part of October Term 2024 until the new term starts on Monday, October 6, 2025.

The Court usually grants review in about half of the cases on a term's docket before it adjourns for the summer. It continues to take cases until the middle of January, which will be decided by the end of June. And, of course, as was true in October Term 2024, the Court can take emergency matters. For example, the Court heard oral arguments in *Trump v. CASA*, the case about birthright citizenship and nationwide injunctions, on May 15, 2025.[1]

The Court has a number of likely significant cases that will be heard and decided in October Term 2025. These are some of the higher-profile cases.

Louisiana v. Callais

The Supreme Court had briefing and oral argument in *Louisiana v. Callais* in October Term 2024, but then to everyone's surprise it did not decide the case. Instead, on June 27, it announced that the case was putting over for new arguments in the coming term. Tradition is that the Court hands down decisions in argued cases by the end of June. But occasionally, the Court has put cases over for reargument. It has done this before in very high-profile cases such as *Brown v. Board of Education*,[2] *Roe v. Wade*,[3] and *Citizens United v. Federal Election Commission*.[4] This reflects that sometimes, in very consequential cases, the Court chooses to take additional time for consideration. *Louisiana v. Callais* has the potential for being such a case.[5]

Section 2 of the Voting Rights Act of 1965 prohibits state and local governments from having election systems or practices that discriminate against minority voters or certain language minority voters. The Voting Rights Act Amendments of 1982 changed the law to provide that proof of racially disparate impact is sufficient for a violation; there does not have to be proof of racially discriminatory intent.

After the 2020 census, Louisiana, like almost every state, redrew its congressional districts. The new districts, adopted by the Louisiana legislature in 2022, had one district with a population that was majority Black individuals out of six congressional districts in the state. In Louisiana, about a third of the population is Black. A three-judge federal district court found this to violate section 2 of the Voting Rights Act because of the racially discriminatory impact in disadvantaging Black voters.

In response to the court's decision, the Louisiana legislature, in 2024, adopted new congressional districts, with two of six having majority Black individuals in their populations. A group of individuals who identified themselves as non-minority voters brought a challenge, contending that Louisiana had violated equal protection. In cases such as *Shaw v. Reno*[6] and *Miller v. Johnson*,[7] the Court held that the government cannot use race as a predominant factor in drawing election districts unless it meets strict scrutiny. The district court ruled in favor of the plaintiffs, finding a violation of equal protection, but the Supreme Court stayed the district court's order and allowed the new districts, with two majority Black districts, to be used in the 2024 elections.

The Court granted review on several questions: "(1) Whether the majority of the three-judge district court in this case erred in finding that race predominated in the Louisiana legislature's enactment of S.B. 8; (2) whether the majority erred in finding that S.B. 8 fails strict scrutiny; (3) whether the majority erred in subjecting S.B. 8 to the preconditions specified in *Thornburg v. Gingles*; and (4) whether this action is non-justiciable."

The Court did not decide these questions, but instead announced it will hear the case again next term. Justice Thomas, though, dissented from having the matter reargued and made clear that he would hold that allowing disparate impact liability under section 2 of the Voting Rights Act violates equal protection. Justice Thomas wrote that the Voting Rights Act and the requirements of equal protection are "in tension."[8] Section 2 of the Voting Rights Act effectively requires that race be considered in drawing election districts to ensure that there is not a racially disparate impact against minority voters. But under *Shaw v. Reno* and *Miller v. Johnson*, it violates equal protection for race to be used as a predominant consideration in districting.

Justice Thomas left no doubt that he believes that this makes section 2 of the Voting Rights Act unconstitutional. He stated: "These cases put the Court to a choice: It may permit patent racial gerrymandering under the auspices of §2 compliance, or it may admit that, as the Court has construed the statute, a violation of §2 is insufficient to justify a race-based remedy. That decision should be straightforward. Nevertheless, the Court demurs."[9]

The implications of Justice Thomas' position—if it is accepted by a majority of the Court—are enormous. It would mean that disparate impact liability under section 2 of the Voting Rights Act would be unconstitutional, at least in situations where it requires decision-makers to consider race. That in itself would be dramatic and change the nature of the political system in the United States. But the implications could extend beyond that. Other federal laws, such as Title VII in prohibiting employment discrimination and the Fair Housing Act of 1968 also create liability based on disparate impact. Would those be constitutionally vulnerable as well because avoiding disparate impact requires decision-makers to consider race?

In 2009, in a concurring opinion in *Ricci v. DeStefano*, a case involving employment discrimination, Justice Antonin Scalia raised the issue of whether disparate impact liability violates equal protection.[10] He said in that case the Court was just "postpone[ing] the evil day on which the Court will have to confront the question: Whether, or to what extent, are the disparate-impact provisions of Title VII of the Civil Rights Act of 1964 consistent with the Constitution's guarantee of equal protection? . . . [I]f the Federal Government is prohibited from discriminating on the basis of race, then surely it is also prohibited from enacting laws mandating that third parties—*e.g.*, employers, whether private, State, or municipal—discriminate on the basis of race."[11] He said that "the war between disparate impact and equal protection will be waged sooner or later.[12]

On August 1, the Supreme Court issued an order for additional briefing that left no doubt that the constitutionality of section 2 of the Voting Rights Act is before it. The Court's order stated: "The parties are directed to file supplemental briefs addressing the following question raised [in that brief]: Whether the State's intentional creation of a second majority-minority congressional district violates the Fourteenth or Fifteenth Amendments to the U.S. Constitution." The case thus could have huge implications for the Voting Rights Act and, indeed, all civil rights laws, as the Supreme Court is considering the constitutionality of disparate impact liability.

It is impossible to overstate the importance of disparate impact liability to enforcing civil rights in the United States. For a half century, the Supreme Court has held that proving that there is a racial classification for purposes of equal protection requires demonstrating that the government had a discriminatory intent. But rarely any longer do legislators or government decision-makers openly express a racist purpose. Also, social psychologists long have documented that people have implicit biases that influence their decisions, but that are not acknowledged or openly stated. That is why civil rights statutes creating liability upon proof of a racially disparate impact are so important. *Louisiana v. Callais* presents to the Court the issue in the context of a vitally important civil rights law: section 2 of the Voting Rights Act.

Chiles v. Salazar

One of the themes of this book is how the culture wars have come to the U.S. Supreme Court. There are a number of cases presenting "culture war" issues on the docket for the October 2025 Term. *Chiles v. Salazar* involves the constitutionality of a Colorado law that prohibits "conversion therapy"—that is, it prohibits efforts to try and change a person's sexual orientation or gender identity.[13] The Colorado law forbids "any practice or treatment by licensee, registrant, or certificate holder that attempts or purports to change an individual's sexual orientation or gender identity, including efforts to change behaviors or gender expressions or to eliminate or reduce sexual or romantic attraction or feelings toward individuals of the same sex." But anyone "engaged in the practice of religious ministry" is exempt from complying with the law.

Kaley Chiles brought a lawsuit challenging the Colorado law and claiming that it violates her freedom of speech and free exercise of religion. She says that she is a licensed counselor and a practicing Christian. She argues that the law violates her right to counsel clients. The U.S. Court of Appeals for the Tenth Circuit ruled against Chiles and upheld the Colorado law.[14] The court stressed the "long-established history of states regulating the healthcare professions."[15] The court found that only rational basis review is appropriate and concluded that Colorado's interests in protecting children were sufficient to uphold the law.

It will be interesting to see how the Court handles this case in light of its decision in *United States v. Skrmetti*, which is discussed in Chapter 8.[16] In that case, the Court stressed the need for deference to the Tennessee legislature in deciding how to best protect transgender children. Will the Supreme Court show similar deference to the Colorado legislature in its prohibition of conversion therapy?

Little v. Hecox and *West Virginia v. B.P.J.*

Few issues are more divisive, or more reflect the culture wars, than whether transgender athletes can participate in sports that correspond with their gender identities. Yet for all the attention, this is about a relatively small number of people. In December 2024, the President of the National Collegiate Athletic Association, Charlie Baker, told a Senate committee that there are fewer than ten transgender athletes in college sports out of 510,000 collegiate athletes.

The two cases before the Supreme Court involve laws in Idaho and West Virginia that prohibit transgender athletes from competing in sports that correspond to their gender identities. Idaho, in 2020, adopted a law prohibiting transgender athletes from competing in sports. Lindsay Hecox, a transgender woman who wanted to try out for the Boise State University women's track and cross-country teams, challenged the law as violating equal protection and also Title IX of the federal civil rights law that prohibits educational institutions receiving federal funds from discriminating based on sex. The federal district court ruled in her favor, and that decision was affirmed by the U.S. Court of Appeals for the Ninth Circuit.[17]

The other case involves, B.P.J., a transgender 14-year-old girl who challenged a West Virginia statute prohibiting transgender athletes from competing in sports that correspond to their gender identities. B.P.J. says that she has publicly identified as a girl since the third grade, takes medicine to prevent male puberty, and has begun to receive hormone therapy with estrogen. She, too, sued under equal protection and Title IX, with the U.S. Court of Appeals for the Fourth Circuit ultimately ruling in her favor based on Title IX.[18]

In *Skrmetti*, the Court did not decide the level of scrutiny to be used for gender identity discrimination. That is sure to be before the Court in these cases. Also, there is the question of how to interpret Title IX and its prohibition against sex discrimination. In *Bostock v. Clayton County, Georgia*, the Supreme Court held that the prohibition of sex discrimination in employment applies to gender identity discrimination.[19] Will the Court say the same for Title IX? How will the Court deal with the State's argument that it should be able to protect girls' and women's sports by excluding transgender women, as opposed to the claim of the plaintiffs that this is discrimination based on gender identity that violates equal protection and Title IX?

Religious Land Use and Institutionalized Persons Act

In *Employment Division v. Smith*, the Supreme Court held that the free exercise clause cannot be used to challenge a neutral law of general applicability.[20] Congress then enacted the Religious Freedom Restoration Act (RFRA) to, by statute, restore protection of religious freedom to what it was prior to *Employment Division v. Smith*. It provides that the government must meet strict scrutiny when it substantially burdens religion. But in *City of Boerne v. Flores*, the Supreme Court declared that the RFRA was unconstitutional as applied to state and local governments as exceeding the scope of Congress's powers.[21]

Congress then adopted the Religious Land Use and Institutionalized Persons Act (RLUIPA). It provides that state and local governments must meet strict scrutiny if they substantially burden religion in their land use decisions or in their treatment of institutionalized persons.

The issue in *Landor v. Louisiana Department of Corrections & Public Safety* is whether government officials can be sued for money damages for violating RLUIPA.[22] Damon Landor, a devout Rastafarian, adhered to a Nazarite vow to grow his hair.[23] During his incarceration in 2020, two previous facilities respected this vow, with one even amending its grooming policy for him. With only three weeks left in his sentence, Landor was transferred to Raymond Laborde Correctional Center (RLCC).

Upon arrival, he informed the intake guard of his religious practice, provided proof of past accommodations, and even gave a copy of a Fifth Circuit decision that found Louisiana's policy of cutting Rastafarian hair violated the RLUIPA. The guard discarded his papers and summoned Warden Marcus Myers, who demanded documentation from Landor's sentencing judge. When Landor could not immediately produce it, two guards handcuffed him to a chair, held him down, and shaved his head.

After his release, Landor sued the Louisiana Department of Corrections, the prison, Warden Myers, and Secretary James LeBlanc in their individual and official capacities. His claims included violations under RLUIPA and 42 U.S.C. § 1983 (for First, Eighth, and 14th Amendment violations), as well as state law claims. Myers and LeBlanc moved to dismiss the RLUIPA claims against them in their individual capacities, arguing such claims were barred by precedent. The district court agreed, dismissing these claims on the grounds that RLUIPA "does not authorize a private cause of action for compensatory or punitive damages."[24] Landor then appealed this dismissal.

The U.S. Court of Appeals for the Fifth Circuit affirmed the district court's dismissal. The court explicitly held that RLUIPA does not provide for money damages against officials sued in their individual capacities.[25]

In *Tanzin v. Tanvir*, the Supreme Court allowed suits for money damages against federal officials in their individual capacities under the Religious Freedom Restoration Act.[26] The Fifth Circuit found that case inapplicable to RLUIPA and the Supreme Court has granted review to determine whether such suits for monetary relief can be brought under this important federal statute.

Fourth Amendment

It has been several years since the Supreme Court has decided a case about searches under the Fourth Amendment. *Case v. Montana* poses the question of whether law enforcement may enter a home with a search warrant based on less than probable cause that an emergency is occurring, or whether the emergency aid exception requires probable cause.[27]

In *Brigham City, Utah v. Stuart*, the Court held that the police may enter a home without a warrant when they have an objectively reasonable basis for believing that an occupant is seriously injured or imminently threatened with such injury.[28] But does this require "probable cause" to believe there is such a danger? The Supreme Court has recognized a "community caretaking" exception to the warrant requirement, but when does it apply?[29]

After a report from his ex-girlfriend that William Trevor Case had threatened suicide, police officers went to his home. After waiting about 40 to 45 minutes, the officers entered the house. A police officer who encountered Case in an upstairs bedroom believed that he saw a "dark object" near Case's waist and fired at him, hitting him in the left arm and lower left abdomen.

Case was arrested and moved to suppress the evidence the police gained, claiming that the entry to his house was illegal. The trial court denied his suppression motion and he was convicted. The Montana Supreme Court affirmed, finding that the community caretaking exception was sufficient to allow the police entry without violating the Fourth Amendment.[30]

National Republican Senatorial Committee v. Federal Election Commission[31]

In *Federal Election Commission v. Colorado Republican Federal Campaign Committee*, in 2001, the Court held provisions in federal law that limited coordinated campaign expenditures between political parties and the candidates.[32] In *National Republican Senatorial Committee v. Federal Election Commission*, the Court is being asked to decide whether the changes in the law of campaign finance in the last quarter century warrant overruling the earlier decision and whether the Court should find that it violates the First Amendment for the government to prohibit coordinated expenditures between a political party and a candidate.

Conclusion

These, of course, are only some of the cases already on the docket for October Term 2025, with many more to be added. There is no doubt that the Court also will have many matters—certainly on the emergency docket and perhaps on the merits docket—that involve challenges to the Trump administration's actions.

My hope is that at a time when the country is so deeply divided and there is a President repeatedly challenging constitutional boundaries, the Court can play a checking role and even find ways to unify the country. This was not what the Court did in October 2024, as instead it very much took sides.

Endnotes

1. Trump v. CASA, 145 S. Ct. 2540 (2025).
2. 347 U.S. 483 (1954).
3. 410 U.S. 113 (1973).
4. 558 U.S. 310 (2010).
5. No. 24-109.
6. 509 U.S. 630 (1993).
7. 515 U.S. 900 (1995).
8. 145 S. Ct. 2608, 2610 (Thomas, J., dissenting).
9. *Id.* at 2612.
10. 557 U.S. 557 (2009).
11. *Id.* at 594 (Scalia, J., concurring).
12. *Id.* at 595–96.
13. No. 24-539.

14. 116 F.4th 1178 (10th Cir. 2024).
15. *Id.* at 1206.
16. 145 S. Ct. 1816 (2025).
17. 104 F.4th 1061 (9th Cir. 2024).
18. 98 F.4th 542 (4th Cir. 2024).
19. 590 U.S. 644 (2020).
20. 494 U.S. 872 (1990).
21. 521 U.S. 507 (1997).
22. No. 23-1197.
23. Landor v. Louisiana Dep't of Corr. & Pub. Safety, 82 F.4th 337, 339 (5th Cir. 2023).
24. Landor v. Louisiana Dep't of Corr. & Pub. Safety, No. CV 21-733-SDD-SDJ, 2022 WL 4593085 at *2 (M.D. La. Sept. 29, 2022).
25. *Id.* 82 F.4th 337 (5th Cir. 2023).
26. 592 U.S. 43 (2020).
27. No. 24-624.
28. 547 U.S. 398 (2006).
29. Caniglia v. Strom, 141 S. Ct. 1596 (2021).
30. 553 P.3d 985 (Mont. 2024).
31. No. 24-621.
32. 533 U.S. 431 (2001).

Index